A CSIS STORY

*How the Service Treated One
Intelligence Officer Candidate Application*

Paul Deslauriers

and

Krzysztof Piotrowski

*This book is dedicated to the men and women in the
business of protecting our country's security and freedoms
who know what they're doing. May they have the wisdom
the recognize a loyal ally when they see one.*

CONTENTS

INTRODUCTION

On August 14, 2019, the CBC broadcasted and posted a story online titled "Recruitment, retention 'issues of concern' for CSIS: internal docs". The article was based on a briefing package for the Canadian Security Intelligence Service (CSIS) Director which was released pursuant to an *Access to Information Act* request. The article suggested that there was a recruitment and retention problem at CSIS and that "A hiring slump could have implications for how CSIS operates as it collects and analyzes intelligence on threats to Canada's national security."

What was the key problem according to the article? "Most former CSIS employees who spoke to CBC News said one of the main issues in keeping employees is the mobility clause." National security investigations may happen anywhere across the country. CSIS headquarters, like most federal Government bureaucracies, is located in Ottawa. However, CSIS also has numerous field offices across the country and Intelligence Officers will typically rotate and change positions at some point in their careers to include stints at headquarters and in the field. Many of these "tours of duty" are temporary. Not surprisingly, applicants who make it through the application process and are offered a position as an Intelligence Officer with CSIS are required to agree to relocate anywhere across Canada. Notwithstanding these facts, the story further provided that "Michel Juneau–Katsuya, a former CSIS senior official and manager at CSIS, stated that 'Last I heard, they would lose an average of 30 percent [of employees] within the first five years.'"

Thirty percent of people who join CSIS quit within five years? And a major reason is that they don't want to move? Given that CSIS makes it clear to all recruits that the job involves the possibility of moving, why would CSIS hire, train and invest in people who were not willing to meet one of the basic requirements of the job and stick around for more than five years? Thirty percent of new hires leaving within five years is a lot. It may not be as high as the staff turnover at the local coffee shops, but it's a serious problem. Imagine what the staffing headache would be like at Global Affairs Canada if 30% of the "Foreign Service Officers" that were hired and trained to staff Canada's diplomatic corps and missions around the world decided to quit when they were told what their first diplomatic post assignment was?

Recruiting, training and integrating new officers into the Service is a costly endeavour. Besides being a significant drain on resources, the loss of significant numbers of personnel must inevitably have a disruptive effect on operations. While fast food franchises can handle it, national security investigations and operations are rarely fast and often take years. How does senior management at CSIS feel about the loss of personnel who are trained in CSIS spycraft walking around with all their knowledge and no longer under the control of their former employer? How comfortable and secure are they that their former employees will keep their lips zipped? All it takes is one person to spoil an operation. It must be a constant source of worry. Thirty percent within five years? No one can tell the future, but perhaps CSIS is not picking its recruits very well.

Krzysztof Piotrowski is an acquaintance whom I met years ago when we were starting our careers as civil servants in the federal Government bureaucracy. Krzysztof will usually introduce himself as Christopher, or Chris for short, except when meeting fellow Poles. Piotrowski has been a kind friend over the years and I always enjoyed our discussions about history and politics. He often has an interesting perspective and assessment of past and current events.

He also enjoys hearing and discussing other perspectives. Both of us have learned from each other over the years. Our conversations about world politics would occasionally steer towards issues of national security. On one occasion years ago, Piotrowski told me that he had some experience dealing with CSIS. He had applied to be an "Intelligence Officer" and went through the recruitment process and was rejected at the tail end. After he told me this he shrugged and said that they probably did him a favour and switched the topic of the conversation.

However, after seeing the CBC story I raised the issue with Piotrowski again. This time he was more forthcoming and told me about his experience. He applied to CSIS after law school. He went through all the tests and interviews. He thought they were relatively easy and straightforward. He wondered when would there be a hard part? It never came. The final panel interview with three senior CSIS officials was supposed to be hard, but Piotrowski walked out of there wondering "Is that it?" He waited as CSIS did a background security check on him. When he called the head of recruiting to inquire about the status of his application, he was told that the only thing left was to get the security clearance. As Piotrowski could think of no reason to deny him a security clearance, he waited.

And waited.

And then one day he got a rejection form letter in the mail.

By that time Piotrowski had begun to suspect that the length of time CSIS was taking to conclude its investigation into his background was a sign of a problem. However, there was no indication of what the problem was. Just a standard form letter saying "thank you for your interest and have a nice day".

Piotrowski decided to apply under the *Privacy Act* for a copy of his CSIS application file. Piotrowski explained that when he got the package in the mail it was eye-opening and troubling. He did not go into details and instead said *"They're a bunch of incompetent jerks. Their investigation and analysis of my background was remarkably amateurish and looked like a half-baked history project by some adolescents. There were so many errors, misinterpretations and omissions that it cured me of whatever previous respect I had for CSIS. One of their investigators spent over four hours interviewing me and then wrote a report suggesting that I might be a spy."*

Piotrowski thought he would be able to contribute to the defence and protection of Canada's liberties and freedoms. He had previously held the Service in high esteem, but after seeing the hatchet job they did on his application file he realized that his admiration for the Service and desire to devote his career to it were unwarranted and seriously misguided. He regretted that he previously developed an interest in national security matters and wanted to pursue a career with CSIS. Canada's freedom, Piotrowski would say, *"was not thanks to CSIS but in spite of it."* He no longer had any confidence or trust in the organization and those who worked there.

Piotrowski then revealed to me that he had two boxes full of notes and files in his attic. I asked him if he ever thought of writing a book about his experience. He responded that in the period after CSIS rejected his candidacy he was preoccupied with getting a career going, pursuing a third degree, and starting a family. Book writing about this unpleasant experience of rejection and failure was not on his agenda. However, in subsequent years he came across three new books that confirmed to him that his negative experience and impression of CSIS was not unique but reflective of a second-rate outfit.

One day in 2000 while browsing in a bookstore, Piotrowski spotted a thin book with a red cover by a former CSIS officer named William Baltruweit. The book was titled *Down and Out in Canada's Intelligence Service: How CSIS Used Counter-Intelligence Techniques to Investigate a Depressed Employee.* Chris bought the book and found it a fascinating account by someone in the Service who had been depressed. CSIS treated him in such a shameful way that he was out of the Service and wrote a book that was hardly complimentary to CSIS. After his own application debacle, Piotrowski had no problems envisioning the experience Baltruweit described in his book.

A few years later Piotrowski came across Andrew Mitrovica's book *Covert Entry - Spies, Lies and Crimes Inside Canada's Security Service*

(2003). The stories in that book were about an undercover agent's experience with CSIS. To say that the book made CSIS employees and management appear to be untrustworthy and considerably less than honourable folk would be an understatement. Integrity did not appear to be a CSIS value. Piotrowski said he found reading that book a tremendous source of relief. Although he previously felt a sense of failure at his having been rejected by CSIS, Mitrovica's book transformed the sting of failure into a sense of gratitude for being sparred the unwanted experience of embarking on a lifetime journey with such a lamentable organization.

The third in this divulgence trilogy of Keystone Cops installments was J. Michael Cole's *Smokescreen* (2008). Cole had joined CSIS and then quit the organization after a few short years and wrote a treatise that was stunning in its critique of practically every aspect of the Service. Piotrowski remarked that the number of times the words "incompetent" and "ignorant" came up in the book was so frequent he was surprised they were not in the book's subtitle. One of the issues that Cole repeatedly raised throughout his book was the laziness and shortcuts that CSIS employees routinely demonstrated in the process of applications for warrants and related renewals.

Do things change over time? According to a media story twelve years later, a review was held of CSIS' procedures for obtaining a warrant and found that "*...ineffective training, excessive secrecy and a generally poor understanding of responsibilities contributed to CSIS failing...*" ("CSIS sees warrant process as 'burdensome' and a 'necessary evil': federal review", *CBC*, October 13, 2020).

After reading these books Piotrowski eventually came to consider the idea of writing a book about his own experiences a possibility. I asked Piotrowski if he would be willing to get the boxes out of the attic and write a book with me about his experiences. He agreed, provided that I did most of the writing! Throughout the book *italics* are used where Piotrowski is quoted.

The story in this book is about one young, educated and energetic Canadian's desire to join CSIS and how CSIS treated his application, and him. The story reveals much about CSIS at the time. Hopefully,

CSIS will have improved its procedures and the quality of its investigations and analysis since the period when it rejected Chris' application. But perhaps not. Judging by recent media headlines CSIS seems to have a steady crop of human resource "issues": "Fired CSIS agent with mental health issues suing the federal government" (*Ottawa Citizen*, August 22, 2016); "CSIS faces $35-million harassment, discrimination lawsuit" (*Globe and Mail*, July 14, 2017); and "A 'second class' spy: Muslim CSIS agent alleges discrimination, abuse" (*CBC*, January 21, 2020).

This book reflects Piotrowski's version of the story and the reader will no doubt keep in mind that CSIS has its own version. The individuals at CSIS with whom Piotrowski came into contact obviously had their own perspectives and interpretations. The internal documents which Piotrowski received as a result of his *Privacy Act* request certainly made that clear. However, CSIS most likely destroyed all relevant files years ago and whatever memory its employees had likely faded away or was lost upon retirement. Piotrowski emphasizes that in reviewing the CSIS side of things, one has to keep the following in mind. In one meeting with CSIS' "Chief Psychologist", when Piotrowski asked if he could take notes of what he was being told, the Chief Psychologist responded by saying that Piotrowski could make whatever notes he wanted, but if the matter ended up in court, he would *"deny everything"*. Clearly, lying under oath and committing the criminal offense of perjury is not an issue for some people at CSIS.

Hopefully, most of the CSIS personnel that Piotrowski had to deal with have since retired and a new crop of employees may be more enlightened. After three decades CSIS must have evolved and changed. What organization hasn't? However, some elements of the story may still resonate today.

This book should be of interest to anyone interested in CSIS and how such secret bureaucracies operate. They have their own culture and modus operandi. Anyone considering making an application to CSIS may benefit from reading this. It may make them question their reasons for wanting to apply and may provide some valuable lessons.

This story should also be a source of amusement to those who enjoy reading about bureaucratic red tape and incompetence. Piotrowski claims that what used to be a source of disappointment and grief now provokes chuckles. How times change.

LIST OF CHARACTERS

Maria Adamska. Krzysztof Piotrowski's mother.

Harry Brandes. Deputy Director, Intelligence (DDI) at CSIS.

Debbie Cavana. Head, Acquisitions and Serials Management, CSIS Information Centre.

General Antoine de Fougerolles. Head of the International Security Institute (ISI).

Stewart Duncan. Veteran RCMP/CSIS officer on contract conducting security screening investigations.

Sylvain Gagner. A friend of Piotrowski in Calgary.

Vincent Gendron. CSIS Psychology Unit member.

Jean Goblet. Senior CSIS official and member of the final interviewing panel.

Julia Goodale. Internal Security officer and interviewer.

Victor Goulet. CSIS officer in Personnel department, recruiting unit.

Desmond Greywood. Officer in the Communications Unit.

Suzanne Guibault. French language teacher on contract at CSIS.

Larry Finch. Chief "psychologist" at CSIS.

Ted D'Arcy Finn. First Director of CSIS (1984-1987).

Serge Fortin. Senior CSIS official and member of the final interviewing panel.

Stewart Fowler. CSIS Officer from the Montreal regional office.

Hon. Bob Kaplan, PC, MP. Former Solicitor-General of Canada responsible for the passage of the *CSIS Act*.

W.H. Kelly. Former Deputy Commissioner of the RCMP.

Richard Latrappe. CSIS Personnel Department. Head of Recruiting.

Barry Lemmings. Chief of CSIS Communications Unit.

Col. Liam McNabb. Head of the Institute of Strategic Studies (ISS).

Reid Morden. CSIS Director (1988 – 1992).

David Onions. CSIS officer. First interviewer of candidate applicants.

Stanisław Piotrowski. Krzysztof Piotrowski's father.

John Starnes. Director of the RCMP Security Service (1970-1973).

Dave Thompson. RCMP/CSIS veteran with experience in "counter-subversion".

CHAPTER 1:
THE MAKING OF
A CSIS CANDIDATE

Chris Piotrowski's parents were Polish immigrants who came to Canada in 1960. Piotrowski was born in Montreal a few years later. Piotrowski's father, Stanisław Piotrowski, was a professor of philosophy at McGill University in Montreal. He had studied law (LL.M.) in Poland and earned a Ph.D. in Philosophy. His specialty was logic. Once Chris was old enough, discussions with his father were always subjected to the critical analysis of a logician. Chris often found talking with his father and sharing ideas that came to mind to be frustrating, as his father would inevitably question the basis of assertions that were on shaky foundations and detect fallacies in Chris' reasoning. Discussions often concluded by highlighting what one could and couldn't say with certainty on any given topic. Chris noted when visiting friends that none of their discussions around the dinner table involved such frequent and detailed dissections of propositions and hypotheses.

For several years, Piotrowski's father was the chairman of the philosophy department. This kept him busy with teaching and administration responsibilities. Whatever free time he had was frequently spent in the Polish ethnic community. His father was active in the Polish Canadian Congress and spent endless hours on the phone and in meetings.

Piotrowski's father was a liberal democrat and an unabashed anti-communist. He had experience with Stalinism. Piotrowski's paternal grandfather was among the Polish officers captured by the Soviets when they invaded Poland in September 1939 and divided the country with Hitler. His grandfather was among the thousands of Polish prisoners executed in 1940 by the NKVD, on orders from Stalin, in what became known as the Katyn Forest Massacre. The Katyn war crime deeply affected Polish society, and especially all the families who lost loved ones. Many of the families of the victims who lived in the Soviet occupation zone were rounded up in midnight arrests and deported in cattle cars to Siberia. From the Polish perspective, Katyn and the deportations were further evidence of the cruelty of the Soviets.

Piotrowski's father dreamed of a free Poland no longer in the Soviet empire. He had no idea if it would happen in his lifetime, but he was confident that if America stayed strong, the West would prevail and win the Cold War. The Soviet system was unsustainable and bankrupt.

In his youth, Chris was taught about the differences between Soviet totalitarian communism and Western liberal democracy. As a young boy, Chris did not fully appreciate the teachings of his father. However, when he visited his distant relatives in Poland during the 1970s he came to appreciate the significance of what his father had tried to explain to him.

Piotrowski's mother survived tremendous hardship as a child in Poland during the war. After the war his mother attended university and studied psychology and sociology at the graduate level, eventually earning two M.A. degrees. She told her son that after all the trauma and stress of the war, she enjoyed the quiet and peaceful pursuit of university studies. However, she never made a career in either of those fields and advised her son when he went to university to avoid sociology and psychology courses which she subsequently considered useless.

Piotrowski's parents enjoyed summer vacations and trips throughout North America and Europe. Chris remembers spending the summer of 1969 in the backseat of his father's convertible Pontiac *Parisenne* as they saw the geysers in Yellowstone, leaned over the edge of the Grand Canyon, and walked up the steps of pyramids in Mexico. Piotrowski remembers his first trip to Paris when he was eight years old and returning to school with a little replica Eiffel Tower that he kept on this school desk.

Piotrowski's father's position at McGill provided him with an opportunity to take a sabbatical every seven years. In 1968, when Piotrowski was six, the family moved for a year to Edmonton where his father worked on a book with another Polish professor at the University of Alberta. Piotrowski attended grade one in a French immersion program at the time. He still keeps in touch with one of my former classmates from that year. The family then returned to Montreal where his parents registered him in a private French lycée school in the Outremont neighbourhood. Within a few years, he spoke French with ease and enjoyed being able to imitate the contrasting accents of his European teachers and Quebec classmates.

Piotrowski's parents separated when he was a kid and later divorced before he reached his teens. His mother reverted to her maiden name, Maria Adamska. At first, Chris lived with his mother in an apartment not far from the Lycée. One of his classmates lived across the street. Fifty years later they are still in touch. His mother then moved to Ottawa and Chris went with her. In Ottawa, he attended an English public school. At the school, Piotrowski met a classmate of German background named Karl. They quickly became friends and frequently referred to each other as brothers. They have been friends ever since.

When Piotrowski's father had his second sabbatical, he took Chris with him to London, England. His father had him try the entrance exams to Westminster School, a private boarding school which is located next door to Westminster Abbey. It was a distinguished school with several centuries of history. Besides catering to the British elite, the school's alumni included some of the biggest names in the history of communism and Nazism. Kim Philby (the notorious traitor and KGB spy) and Rudolf von Ribbentrop (son of Joachim von Ribbentrop who was at the time Hitler's Ambassador to Britain) were among the alumni. After attending a special "cramming" school that prepared students for such entrance exams, Piotrowski endured two days of exams and interviews and was successful. After the summer break, Piotrowski's father returned to teaching in Montreal. His mother moved from Ottawa to Calgary. And Chris began high school in London.

I began my studies at Westminster across the Atlantic from my parents. They had expectations of my completing high school there and attending Oxford or Cambridge. It did not work out that way. I felt like I was in an orphanage at Westminster. We had school six days a week and after class on Saturdays everyone went home, except a handful of students like me with parents who were too far away to visit. I felt abandoned by my parents. I also felt alienated from the majority of my classmates. Even though I spoke the language, I did not have much in common with them. My accent resulted in me being called either a yank or a colonist. I found watching soccer on the tube boring compared to watching hockey. Not surprisingly, I became depressed. My marks dropped in all subjects except French. My best friend there was an American of Norwegian descent. I remember going to several rock concerts with him. The first one was the Rolling Stones. By the end of the year I couldn't wait to go home. As soon as I saw my father at the Montreal airport, I begged him to let me stay in Montreal and forget about London. Fortunately, he readily agreed. After all these years I still keep in touch with two of my Westminster classmates.

Although Piotrowski's parents refused to return to Poland while it was still under Soviet occupation, his father made arrangements for him to visit relatives in Poland on three separate trips in the mid-1970s. Piotrowski met his relatives and experienced what living was like in a country under Soviet domination.

It was eye-opening. There were shortages, lines, lack of basic consumer goods and everything else except, evidently, supplies for the Communist Party members, military, and secret police. The most common word was "niema" which means "there isn't any". It was a common refrain of all the store staff standing by empty shelves. There was a lot of poverty. There were also two different societies. In terms of economics, there was the official one full of "niema", and then the black market where you could get stuff, often with U.S. dollars. In terms of news and official state pronouncements, there was the official narrative, and then the truth which people would only whisper in private. It was a society of deceit in which knowing how to get things done meant knowing who to bribe. Health and dental care were supposed to be free, but everyone knew that you had to pay a "tip". Corruption was the name of the game and the only way that the system "worked". I frequently saw soldiers walking in pairs on sidewalks with machine guns. Why? Who was threatening to attack? I saw police stopping young people randomly and demanding ID for no apparent reason. And there was the monotony and monopoly of endless propaganda. It was everywhere. Billboards. Posters. Monuments. The television news was an education of sorts. Every newscast followed the same format. First, there was an announcement about the celebration of an anniversary of one Polish-USSR treaty or another, followed by footage of workers talking about the fulfillment of production quotas. International news began with a report on the annual general meeting of the Communist Party of the U.S.A. At the time I didn't even know there was a Communist Party in the U.S.A. The first time I heard about such a party in America was on Polish TV.

Piotrowski greatly enjoyed the time he spent in the company of family members and regretted that none of his relatives lived in Canada. He also enjoyed the visits to historic sites and the education he received about Polish history, culture and language. One of the unique features of these trips was the education he received about what happened in Poland during WWII and the nature of the post-war Soviet occupation. However, after the third visit he declined further opportunities to visit again.

Waiting in line for bread was hardly a vacation. I'd had enough. I would have to wait to meet the family in Poland again or we'd have to meet elsewhere. These trips taught me a lot about the differences between liberal democracy and communism. Now I understood my father's thinking much better. I was so grateful that I was born in Canada. My next visits to Poland would only occur after the collapse of the iron curtain.

Upon Piotrowski's return to Montreal from London he resumed his high school education at a private school in the Notre-Dame-de-Grâce neighbourhood. Although Piotrowski was the new kid on the block, he made a few close friends. Years later one of Piotrowski's high school friends would ask him to be an usher at his wedding. His friend's parents were well-connected. Prime Minister Mulroney showed up at the wedding and a little later his friend's father was appointed to the Senate.

Piotrowski's focus upon his return to school in Montreal revolved around school and homework. However, when Piotrowski was 15 a family acquaintance who worked in a clothing store downtown asked if he would like a part-time job. The job would require Piotrowski to work Thursday and Friday evenings after school, and Saturdays. Piotrowski's father reluctantly gave his permission and Chris enthusiastically accepted the job offer. He was required to do some basic maintenance, cleaning and deliveries between two stores located downtown. As a result of this job, Chris ended up building up some savings in his bank account. The following summer he was offered another job.

During the summer when I was sixteen some friends of mine who were bartenders at a club on Bishop Street contacted me in a bit of a panic. They desperately needed a busboy to work Thursday, Friday and Saturday nights. The bar closed at 3:00 a.m. They thought I might be a good candidate. I was excited by the prospect, although I would have to resign from the clothing store job. My father knew the two bartenders and again reluctantly gave his permission. It was exhausting physical work. I had to keep three separate bars stocked with supplies, the heaviest being the cases of beer. I worked

Although Piotrowski's father permitted Chris to work at these part-time jobs, he thought that his son would be better off if he stayed home and read books all day. When Piotrowski showed his father his growing bank account statements his father was unimpressed. Piotrowski did not spend the money he earned. He liked the idea of saving his earnings for the future. Unfortunately, at that time neither he nor his father knew anything about investing, so the money just sat in a bank account.

In the late seventies the media began to report on the RCMP engaging in illegal activities and getting into all kinds of hot water. Eventually the Quebec Government established the Keable Commission of Inquiry into RCMP activities in Quebec. The federal Government then created its own McDonald Commission of Inquiry. The media dutifully reported everything they could once the Commissions began holding hearings. There was a time when the nightly television news carried stories about the RCMP having a "Security Service" that did all kinds of secret things in the name of protecting Canada's national security. Piotrowski began to take notice. It was reassuring to know that Canada had some sort of counter-espionage organization that tried to keep tabs on what the Soviets were up to in Canada.

One of Piotrowski's father's close friends in the Polish community in Montreal was a tall and elderly Polish gentleman by the name of Michal Rybikowski. During the second world war he had been an officer of the Polish intelligence in Danzig, Königsberg and Kaunas. From 1941 he created a spy network under the cover of General Makoto Onodery, an employee of the Japanese embassy in Stockholm. Himmler is reported to have described Rybikowski as "the most dangerous officer of Polish intelligence". When Ladislas Farago's bestselling book *The Game of the Foxes* came out in 1971, Chris' father told him that there was a reference to Rybikowski in the book. However, the author did not know Rybikowski's name and referred to him as the "Pesky Pole". On the few occasions that Chris' father would bring Chris along on a visit to Rybikowski's home, the conversation was always about WWII with Rybikowski telling some interesting stories.

After graduating from high school in Montreal Piotrowski set off in September 1980 to the University of Toronto. He was excited to be leaving home and begin his university studies. He shared a room in his college residence with another student. They got along together and kept in touch over the years. Piotrowski's first year roommate would later become a provincial NDP MPP in the Ontario legislature. Piotrowski registered in the Faculty of Arts and Sciences and initially declared economics as his major. Unfortunately, many of the courses that he had registered for (e.g., calculus, computer science) turned out to be of no interest. Piotrowski thought they would help him in his economics studies, but even the economics classes were so dry and unstimulating that he had a hard time getting motivated to study the material. However, one course that he took was special. The course in political philosophy was his favourite. Professor Thomas Pangle gave inspiring lectures. Piotrowski understood the material and enjoyed the assigned books and readings that were the subjects of class lectures and seminars. He felt energized and excited by that course. Unfortunately, Piotrowski's first year in university turned out to be difficult and academically a failure. The biggest disruption in Piotrowski's first year at university came from women. After having attended private all-boys schools throughout his teens, Piotrowski ended up studying extra-curricular "relationships" which derailed much of his course work. Piotrowski dropped some courses and his marks at the end of year were dreadful, except for the one course in political philosophy.

In the summer of 1981, Piotrowski got a job as a waiter at the Banff Springs Hotel. He lived in the staff quarters. The accommodations and staff cafeteria were inexpensive. Piotrowski managed to live off daily tips and diligently banked his paycheques. He was disciplined about it. He was fortunate to have a job with tips. Over the summer Piotrowski managed to save $2,500. At the time interest rates were over 19% and he then made his first investment by parking his money in a guaranteed investment certificate (GIC).

Piotrowski decided not to return to the University of Toronto. In the Fall of 1981, he moved to Calgary to live with his mother for a while and recharge his batteries before giving university another shot. This was an unhappy and frustrating period of his life. He had decided to give up on the study of economics but did not know what to do.

That first year at U of T was a disaster academically, but an adventure in life and self-discovery. I felt I was on a path of rehabilitation, but I was not quite there yet. I knew that I was going to have to start university over again to get that first degree completed. I just needed to take a breather before giving it another shot. That first year at university made me appreciate the importance of priority-setting, time management and discipline.

While in Calgary Piotrowski had several part-time jobs working in the food service industry at the Palliser Hotel and a number of private clubs. As usual, he accumulated his savings and invested in high interest rate GICs. His parents never asked him to contribute to the housing or food costs at home or for tuition and books when he was at school.

Although Piotrowski was not yet ready to return to university, he decided to enroll in a bartending course offered by the hospitality division of the Southern Alberta Institute of Technology (SAIT) in the fall of 1981. Piotrowski thought it would be helpful to get the course certificate and then apply for some bartending jobs in the city. He thought that throughout his subsequent university studies bartending might prove to be a source of part-time and summer income. Although he ended up getting some working experience later as a bartender, it did not take long before he regretted having wasted his time with the course. The course was about five weeks long. The class size was small with around fifteen students. The course was over by the early afternoon which gave Piotrowski time to work in the late afternoons and evenings in the hotel dining room.

The teacher in the course, Hans Schmidt, was an older man of German background whom Piotrowski thought must have had some Prussian heritage as he conducted his class with military precision. Schmidt was of average height and had a distinct potbelly that made it appear that he had spent an excessive amount of time at the dinner table and bar counter. He gave the impression that he had spent his career tending bar. Having come from Europe he was more knowledgeable about the fine details of alcohol and spirits than most cowboys on the prairies and managed to set himself up in the twilight of his career as a college "professor of mixology". Schmidt ran the program like a thoroughly rehearsed drill sergeant who had set the curriculum in stone a decade earlier would. He was friendly but maintained his professional distance from students.

There were about fifteen other students in the class. They were either high school graduates or dropouts. None had any university background or scholarly ambition. They were either laid off oil rig workers or unemployed drifters who were looking for something that would help them find some easy and casual work. Piotrowski had nothing in common with any of them. Two of the students in the class were particularly rough and looked like unhinged cowboys. Tension developed in the class as it became clear that those two guys up to no good. They frequently appeared to become increasingly drunk throughout the class and people began to suspect that they secretly had a drink or two from the bottles in the classroom bar whenever no one was looking. On several occasions when Piotrowski went to the washroom after class he saw that they were unable to stand straight at the urinals. He suspected that they either had criminal records or were going to get some soon. There were only three young women in the class. One of them made it clear that her life ambition involved marrying her boyfriend who had a truck. Whenever the students in the course took breaks or sat around a table and ate lunch, the conversation was always superficial and meaningless fluff. The attempts at joking and humour on many occasions disintegrated into such silliness that Piotrowski was embarrassed and felt like he was back in high school.

However, there was one student in the bartending class with whom Piotrowski immediately got along at the beginning and became friends with. His name was Sylvain Gagner, and he was about ten years older than Piotrowski was. He was from Quebec, fluently bilingual, and spoke with a distinct Quebecois accent. Piotrowski enjoyed listening to him speaking as it reminded him of Montreal and home. Gagner was normally a happy guy who frequently smiled and said "hello" to everyone. He was a gentle person. However, he was occasionally slow. Somedays he seemed to be terribly sleepy. Other days he was upbeat. Eventually, as the two spent more time together and got to know each other, Gagner told Piotrowski that he was not well. He had some mental health issues, including depression, and was always on medication of one kind or another. Gagner was not employed and was on some sort of welfare disability program. Gagner spent a lot of his free time just walking around Calgary. Although he got along with everyone in the course, nobody else seemed to particularly reach out to be friends with him. After the course ended the two kept in touch and occasionally met to go see a movie or have a beer together. On several occasions Piotrowski invited Gagner to his home for dinner. On more than one occasion Gagner told Piotrowski he was Gagner's best friend and Gagner appreciated the friendship. So did Piotrowski.

As the course progressed Piotrowski grew intellectually bored and was ready to go back to university. He regretted having taken the term off. Nonetheless, on the last day of class Piotrowski attended a party with the students and wished them all good luck.

Years later a CSIS investigator would interview the bartending course instructor as part of the security clearance process. Based on the interview the investigator wrote a report that painted a distorted picture of that brief period in Piotrowski's life. Among other things, the investigator stated that Piotrowski did not get along with anybody. That was not true. Piotrowski's friendship with Gagner was probably the most amicable one among all the students in the course but the instructor either knew nothing about it or opted not to mention it. Similarly, Piotrowski had many friends that he met at every stage of his life, but just not in this small group of people at this particular time. Regrettably, the investigator's report did not provide any context or indicate that this period was probably the bleakest period in Piotrowski's life and hardly reflective of his demeanor before or since. Instead, the investigator's damaging character assassination ended up being repeated over and over again and generalized in subsequent memorandums by "analysts" at CSIS headquarters. In the process, the investigator's report took on an ominous and threatening nature which was magnified by the subsequent repetition throughout the file, the permeation of which made it appear as an unquestionable fact.

In January 1982 Piotrowski resumed his university studies at the University of Calgary where he was put on academic probation. That was an extra incentive to study hard and get good marks. He decided to take some business courses. He particularly enjoyed one introductory course involving group projects relating to the entrepreneurial launching of a business. At the end of the course, each group had to make a presentation to the class as if the group was making a pitch to bankers for financing. Students in each class would vote for the best team presentation. The winning two teams from each class would then compete in a showdown with judges from the private sector. Piotrowski was in a group that eventually won the second overall prize. In the process, he ended up having a romantic relationship with one of the female members of the team and developed a close friendship with an older member of the team who had become the team's *de facto* leader from the beginning. Years later CSIS analysts would write that Piotrowski did not get along in groups. That was not true. Regrettably, the generalization was based on the Calgary investigator's report and the brief and anomalous bartending course experience. Piotrowski's group project classmates were not interviewed.

One of the courses that Piotrowski took in the philosophy department from which he benefitted a great deal was a course on logic. He took the course as he was sure to get an "A" and he needed to raise his average to get off academic probation. Another course that he greatly enjoyed was on the subject of political ideologies. That course was so interesting that Piotrowski decided to switch his major to political science. Piotrowski's marks were improving and by the summer of 1983 he decided to return home to Montreal and finish his undergraduate degree at McGill University.

During this period Piotrowski developed an increasing interest in politics and international relations. Several international developments illustrated the deadly seriousness of the Cold War. While President Carter was promoting human rights and losing influence and allies in places like Iran and Nicaragua, the Soviets were expanding their empire. Revolutions gave way to even more repressive dictatorships. The decade of the 1970s ended with the Soviet invasion of Afghanistan. Reagan's election in 1980 put an end to that trend. The liberation of Grenada, albeit a small island, illustrated the new challenge to the Soviets.

The Soviets had deployed SS-20 missiles in Europe and destabilized the previous balance of power. NATO planned to deploy Cruise and Pershing missiles to restore the balance. The Soviet peace propaganda machine went into overdrive as it tried to promote unilateral disarmament in the West. Although the tactics had been successful in getting Carter to abandon plans for the deployment of the neutron bomb, Reagan stood firm. The deployment of Cruise and Pershing missiles would proceed as planned. However, Reagan was prepared to negotiate the cancellation of the plans if the Soviets would remove their SS–20s, and allow for on–site verification (which the Soviets never previously allowed).

When the Soviets left the negotiation table before the 1984 election the peace movement in the West went hysterical and largely blamed the impasse on the Reagan administration. The peacenik demonstrations always seemed to denounce NATO without any corresponding criticism of the Warsaw Pact missiles aimed at us. Fortunately, Reagan did not falter and believed that the Soviets would return to the negotiation table because it was in their interests to do so. He was right. They came back to the negotiating table before the election when it was clear that Reagan was going to win in a landslide. Reagan not only signed the first INF nuclear disarmament treaty with the Soviets (previous SALT I and II treaties imposed caps but not reductions), he also quarterbacked the West's resistance to Soviet expansionist ambitions and contributed to the eventual crumbling of the Berlin Wall, the Iron Curtain, and the disintegration of the Soviet empire. Piotrowski followed all these developments over the years with interest.

Piotrowski continued his political science studies at McGill in September 1983. One of the courses that Piotrowski took at McGill was modern European history. Although Piotrowski dropped out of the course at the University of Toronto, this time he got the highest mark in his class (95%) and finished with an "A+". He had come a long way since his false start just a few years earlier.

Around this time Piotrowski came to realize that the required readings of his political science courses were merely a minimal list of books that one should be familiar with. He developed a love of visiting used bookstores to get his hands on more and more books that would shed more light on topics of interest. He acquired a growing library of books on the history of political thought, history, and the Cold War. Piotrowski found that they enriched his studies and provided additional sources that he could footnote in many of his term papers in different courses.

Among the intellectually stimulating experiences Piotrowski had at McGill were the discussions and debates relating to political issues.

Discussions with persons holding opposing views were often great learning opportunities. Piotrowski enjoyed listening or reading what their views were, assessing the arguments, and formulating responses that offered a critique of the other arguments while elucidating his own. Sometimes it was with professors. One political science professor made the stunning statement in one class that *"The government of the Soviet Union is perfectly legitimate and the proof is that there is no opposition."* The professor was either not familiar with totalitarian terror or merely trying to provoke a response from his class. Piotrowski asked him whether the political prisoners who were previous and current inhabitants of the Soviet Gulag might be considered "opposition".

Sometimes the debate was with other students, both in class and after class. In October 1983 Piotrowski wrote an essay that was published in the student newspaper about the peace movement and argued that the agitation was promoting unilateral disarmament which was destabilizing and to the Soviet advantage. The essay was half a page and the editors chose to publish an original cartoon with it. Piotrowski was proud when it came out and provoked some discussion among my classmates. However, the following edition had a lengthy rebuttal from an anti-American who poured all the blame for the nuclear threat on the U.S. and included the statement that only those who had a poster of McCarthy on their walls would agree with Piotrowski. Unfortunately, it is not uncommon on university campuses to see the terms "McCarthyist", "fascist" and "right wing extremist" bandied about by the left who tried to discredit and silence opponents through defamatory character assassination. The statement that no one would take Piotrowski's thesis seriously unless they admired Joe McCarthy was an unnecessary cheap shot, but hardly a reason to avoid responding to the main issues about Warsaw Pact and NATO policies. And so began a lengthy exchange between them in the student newspaper. Each new weekly edition would typically carry a response to the previous issue's letter of the other writer. Piotrowski's opponent skillfully criticized America's historic record throughout the Cold War.

Piotrowski learned a lot from his opponent's arguments and from the research he pursued to refute them. Piotrowski enjoyed the intellectual exercise and felt he benefited by engaging in it. While the occasional cheap shots against him were unpleasant to read, they came with the territory of student debate and served as a reminder of the need for thick skin in political debate. Piotrowski prided himself on refraining from *ad hominem* arguments.

Unfortunately, the whole experience, and corresponding discussions and debates, would subsequently be characterized by CSIS in the worst possible light. CSIS investigators and analysts would refer to this episode to suggest that Piotrowski was a right-wing extremist incapable of objectivity and that the McCarthyist label was "appended" to him. Such debate in university was also referred to as evidence to suggest that Piotrowski could not be expected to be a team player at CSIS and would likely engage in "dissent" and be a source of disruption and problems at CSIS.

In November 1984 the *Montreal Gazette* published a letter by someone from Moscow critical of the U.S. arms control policies and used such wording as "*...we in the Soviet Union think that...*". The letter struck Piotrowski as a good example of Soviet propaganda stemming from the Kremlin. Piotrowski wrote a letter to the editor which was published the following week. He pointed out some of the omissions and distortions in the previous Soviet piece. To Piotrowski's surprise, the Moscow spokesperson wrote a response which the *Montreal Gazette* published the following month. Piotrowski was hoping for another intellectually stimulating series of exchanges, but the editors granted the Soviet propagandist the first and last word. CSIS would later refer to his letter to the editor as something suspicious.

Following the tabling of the McDonald Commission report in 1981, the federal Government accepted the recommendation of separating the RCMP Security Service from the police force and creating a new separate civilian security and intelligence agency. In 1984 Solicitor General Robert Kaplan ushered the *Canadian Security Intelligence Service Act* (*CSIS Act*) through Parliament. The new CSIS organization came into existence that year. Of course, all the initial employees were simply RCMP officers sitting at the same desks but leaving their uniforms at home. In 1985 numerous stories in the media indicated that CSIS was seeking "fresh blood" and was on a recruiting drive.

I decided to update my resume and submit an application. I knew from media reports that CSIS was being flooded with thousands of applications. I eventually received a form rejection letter in response. I was not surprised and expected it. Ironically, I was in fact relieved by it as I did not want to disrupt my plans at that time to pursue my university studies at the graduate level. I also thought I would probably have a better chance later.

In the spring of 1985, Piotrowski decided to join the military (infantry) reserves. He genuinely felt a duty to contribute to the national defence of the country. He applied to several reserve units and was accepted by the Royal Montreal Regiment (RMR). Unfortunately, although he met the basic criteria for officer training, he missed the deadline. Accordingly, he was in a group of "private" recruits. Training was on weekends. Those were long and physically draining days. The team of recruits that Piotrowski was with went through all the basic military training courses and perfected their marching drill and rifle-cleaning. The training was physically demanding. Every time Piotrowski returned home from the armoury his muscles were sore for days. The pay was negligible but that was irrelevant. Piotrowski was happy and proud to wear the uniform and be a member of those standing on guard with the Canadian Forces.

Piotrowski graduated from McGill with a B.A. Honours with Distinction (and an A- average) in the Spring of 1985. In Piotrowski's final year of undergraduate studies he decided to apply to law school. He made a concerted effort to prepare for the Law School Admission Test and did well. He ended up going to the first of the law schools that accepted him: Osgoode Hall Law School in Toronto. Moving to Toronto required Piotrowski to resign from the RMR after he completed the introductory military training course.

Piotrowski's girlfriend at the time wanted to move with him to Toronto, so they decided to look for a condominium to purchase.

They found one about a 30-minute walk away from the law school. It was in a less attractive part of town and the price reflected that, but it looked all right. They split the cost. The home cost $42,000, which required $21,000 from both. Piotrowski's girlfriend has been working for years as an accountant and had the cash for her share. Piotrowski used all the money he had saved since he started his part-time jobs as a teenager which amounted to $10,000. His father contributed the remaining portion of $11,000. Piotrowski and his girlfriend owned the condominium with no mortgage. That turned out to be a wise investment at the time as housing prices started to rise dramatically afterward.

Two years later Piotrowski's relationship with his girlfriend deteriorated to the point where they were both happy to call it quits. She returned to Montreal. They negotiated a price for Piotrowski's buying out her half of the condo which at that time was valued at $120,000. Piotrowski had to get a mortgage of $60,000 to finance the purchase. As a result, he rented two rooms out to fellow students to help generate some cash flow to pay the mortgage. When Piotrowski eventually sold the home in 1989 and moved to Ottawa the value had increased to $142,000.

CSIS investigators and analysts would later suggest that Piotrowski's finances were suspicious and that Piotrowski could not account for his financial status. That was not true. Piotrowski's parents supported him while he was a student and he lived by the commonsense rules of frugality, work, save and invest. His decision to invest in a condominium with his girlfriend turned out to be a profitable one.

Piotrowski's relations with his tenants over the two years were amicable and he still keeps in touch with one of them. However, there was one incident that was an unpleasant experience. When one tenant moved out Piotrowski advertised in the student newspaper. A young black male student came to see the room and the home with his parents. It did not take long for Piotrowski to rent the room to the student. However, when he informed the other tenant, a Polish immigrant studying for a medical degree, that a black person would be joining them in the home, the Pole revealed an ugly racist streak and admonished Piotrowski asking "How could you?" The Polish tenant had just paid the monthly rent. Piotrowski immediately gave him back half of it in cash and told him to find himself another place and move out within two weeks.

Piotrowski found his studies at law school to be a wonderful education. He learned more in first year constitutional law about the history of Canadian politics than he did in years of undergraduate political science courses. However, while some courses in first year like contracts, property, and torts can be really stimulating, Piotrowski found other advanced courses like "land use planning" or "administrative law" were the ultimate cures for insomnia. Similarly, while the development of the skill of writing good case summaries (identifying the relevant facts, issue, decision and reasoning) is enjoyable in first year, the seemingly endless preparation of these summaries can become tedious by third year.

Although some professors were clearly experts in their field and delivered amazing and informative lectures about their respective course subjects, there was a group of professors whose personal political biases were pronounced on a regular basis. Some were such left-wingers that one wondered whether one was in the political science department or law school.

Piotrowski had a professor in first year civil procedure class who frequently injected messaging into his lectures about how the whole justice system was rigged by the wealthy bourgeois establishment for their benefit. At the end of the term students had to write a three-hour exam which represented 100% of the course mark. Unlike in undergraduate studies, students could only identify their papers using assigned numbers, and writing their names was forbidden. That was a good thing. The questions in Piotrowski's civil procedure exam were mostly set-ups to denounce the rules of civil procedure as being structured to the advantage of the rich (who had entrenched interests to preserve), at the expense of the poor (who were always exploited and skinned alive by the "system"). On his exam Piotrowski's shoveled as much as he could of the leftist lines about how there's no justice using as many examples as he could from the rules of civil procedure. He got an "A". On the first day of school the following term Piotrowski bumped into the professor in the hallway and thanked him for the "A" that he had given him. The professor's jaw dropped and he replied *"If I'd known it was you, I wouldn't have given it to you."* Piotrowski smiled. He had the professor figured out.

One of Piotrowski's criminal law professors repeatedly stated in class that *"The greatest threat to our civil liberties is the police and CSIS"*. Piotrowski wondered how much that would have made Andrey Vyshinsky convulse in laughter.

Another professor in a labour law course was also a source of memorable quotes. In one class a student remarked that all the cases the students have been reading reflected disputes between employers and employees and he wondered *"Why can't they just get along?"* Piotrowski thought that was a naïve question given that the majority of disputes settle through negotiation. The class readings involved reading court decisions relating to disputes which represented a small percentage of the entire spectrum of the relationship between employers and employees. However, the professor responded by saying *"That's a good question. The problem is private property. We need a revolution and abolish private property."* Piotrowski was stunned. Piotrowski looked around the class to gauge the reaction of the class. No one seemed bothered by this and some students were taking notes. Piotrowski raised his hand and suggested that revolution and abolishment of private property had already been tried in places like Russia and Poland where the government imposed martial law to squash the Solidarity trade union movement and things did not seem to leave the working class better off. The professor replied that not all states that claim to be communist were really communist and moved on to the next item on his lecture agenda.

During this period Piotrowski's interest in Canadian national security matters blossomed. He continued to frequent used books stores and enjoyed visits to the "World's Biggest Bookstore" downtown where the shelves of remaindered books on sale and the collections of history and espionage titles were extensive. He accumulated a significant number of books about history, the Cold War and the history of the KGB and the CIA that were written by academics, journalists, insiders, and defectors. One such book was Jean-Francois Revel's 1983 book *How Democracies Perish* which provided an enlightening discussion of Soviet influence and the tools that the Soviets used, including the manipulation of the peace movement as part of their "struggle for peace". This theme had also been elaborated on by Vladimir Bukovsky in an insightful essay titled "The Peace Movement and the Soviet Union" initially published in *Commentary* in 1982.

One of the most interesting books that Piotrowski acquired at the time was *Dezinformatsia: The Strategy of Soviet Disinformation* by Richard H. Shultz and Roy Godson (1984). The paperback described the Soviet organizational structure for "active measures" and discussed some of the covert techniques including the use of "front organizations", "agents of influence", and "forgeries". What became obvious was that the freedoms in the West, such as those of speech, media, association and assembly, could be used by the Soviets to surreptitiously promote their agendas and interests. Yet, those freedoms did not exist in totalitarian countries. Clearly, the KGB had a wide-open field to play on, whereas the CIA had a much harder time finding opportunities to organize fronts behind the Iron Curtain and plant stories in *Pravda*. Every time Piotrowski heard someone suggest that the Soviets and the Americans were the same and whatever the KGB does the CIA does too, he wondered how would the CIA go about setting up a "Peace Council" front organization in Leningrad that tried to promote unilateral disarmament in the East and the disintegration of the Warsaw Pact while simultaneously praising and justifying NATO at every opportunity?

The *Dezinformatsia* book contained interviews with former East Bloc intelligence officers, including Ladislav Bittman. Piotrowski then acquired Bittman's *The Deception Game* (1972) and *The KGB and Soviet Disinformation: An Insider's View* (1985). Piotrowski found the history and details in the books fascinating. His book collection expanded to include a number of the recently published books about the KGB, the CIA, and the FBI. His initial books on the KGB included Brian Freemantle's *KGB* (1982) and the works of John Barron, *KGB: The Secret Work of Soviet Secret Agents* (1974) and *KGG Today: The Hidden Hand* (1983). In one used bookstore Piotrowski found a small paperback by J. Edgar Hoover titled *Masters of Deceit: The Story of Communism in America and How to Fight It* (1959). He found the chapters on Communist strategy and tactics, particularly infiltration, fronts, espionage and sabotage to be informative and wondered whether any Canadian Government official or institution would ever publish something of a similar nature regarding the threats to Canada's national security and liberal democracy? Another influential book in Piotrowski's library was James L. Tyson's *Target America: The Influence of Communist Propaganda on U.S. Media* (1981).

Piotrowski also made an effort to acquire copies of every Canadian Government document about national security, including the McDonald Commission's multi-volume reports and studies. At one point he called the office of Senator Michael Pitfield and asked if they had an available copy of the Senate Committee report on Bill C-157 titled *Delicate Balance*. Senator Pitfield had chaired the Committee which studied the first CSIS Bill and issued a report in November 1983. Not only did Senator Pitfield's office send Piotrowski a copy of the final report, it also sent him a bound set of the Committee's hearing transcripts.

Piotrowski also collected books written about Canada's national security, including the classic books by John Sawatsky *Men in the Shadows* (1980), *For Services Rendered* (1982), *Gouzenko* (1984), Jeff Sallot *Nobody Said No* (1979), Richard Fidler *RCMP: The Real Subversives* (1978), James Littleton *Target Nation: Canada and the Western Intelligence Network* (1986), and Merrily Weisbord *The Strangest Dream: Canadian Communists, The Spy Trials & the Cold War* (1983). One special category of books that he kept an eye out for were books about the October Crisis and FLQ terrorism, such as Louis Fournier's *F.L.Q.: The Anatomy of an Undergroup Movement* (1984). Piotrowski studied these books, including the Government reports, with a fine-tooth comb.

However, Piotrowski's favourite books were by Soviet defectors and dissidents. He found the books by former Soviet and East Bloc agents particularly interesting, as well as books by political officials. Besides the classics available in used book stores such as Victor Kravchenko's *I Chose Freedom* (1946) and Igor Gouzenko's *This was my Choice* (1948), Piotrowski benefitted from the bumper crop of revealing memoirs that were published at the time. Arkady N. Shevchenko's *Breaking with Moscow* (1985) and Romuald Spasowski's *The Liberation of One* (1986) were revealing contrasts. One was by a senior Soviet diplomat who was a careerist. The other by a senior Polish diplomat who initially had faith in the ideology of communism. However, as both their careers evolved neither could deny the deceit, fraud and bankruptcy of the Soviet system. Books like Ion Mihai Pacepa's *Red Horizons* (1987) and Vladimir Bukovsky's *To Build a Castle: My Life as a Dissenter* (1978) kept Piotrowski reading well into the night.

Piotrowski's bookshelf featured two other classic books that revealed how the Soviet mythology about creating a "classless" society was a fraud. Milovan Djilas's *The New Class: An Analysis of the Communist System* (1957) was a pioneering work in this regard. However, a more up-to-date and detailed examination of the Soviet system was Michael Voslensky's *Nomenklatura: The Soviet Ruling Class* (1984).

Piotrowski's father gave him a credit card which he told Chris to use for emergencies and buying books. The bills went to Piotrowski's father. Every time Piotrowski went to book stores he used it. One day he was at the "World's Biggest Bookstore" and went to the cash with a pile of books. When it came time to pay his credit card did not work. Piotrowski had maxed out his credit limit. Piotrowski's father never said a word to him about it. His father saw that the bills were coming from book stores. He did not mind in the least and was glad that his son was reading.

One day Piotrowski went downtown and stepped inside a modest building on Bathurst Street. The building seemed to be the Toronto headquarters of all things linked to the Communist Party of Canada

(CPC), including their publishing wing and corresponding bookstore. A gentleman near the entrance asked Piotrowski what he wanted. Piotrowski indicated that he was a student interested in acquiring some books about history and politics. Piotrowski hit a goldmine and picked up a bag full of books about the history of the CPC and its leaders (e.g., Tim Buck), books outlining the Communist interpretation and position on several issues, and several books published in Moscow such as *The CIA in the Dock: Soviet Journalists on International Terrorism* (ed. V. Chernyavsky, 1983) and *CIA Target – The USSR* (Nikolai Yakovlev, 1982).

In an open space in the corner of the floor adorned with posters of Lenin and Stalin on the walls, there was a table around which a rather sad-looking group of party workers were having a meal of spaghetti. Piotrowski thought they were probably quiet and averting his eyes because he was a stranger and they were naturally cautious. Piotrowski noticed a number of issues of the Party newspapers on display. He asked if he could have a couple of the most recent issues. Not wanting to appear overly enthusiastic and give away his attempt at vacuuming up whatever literature he could get, he picked up a few of the issues and after glancing at the front-page headlines he replaced some of them on the shelf. It turned out that the person who showed Piotrowski the catalogue of available books was involved in the production of the Party newspaper and asked Piotrowski if he would like to write for it. Piotrowski said he was really busy with his studies at the time but would consider it. Of course, the chances of that ever happening were non-existent.

Besides acquiring and devouring his growing book collection, Piotrowski found and copied relevant journal articles in the university library. Piotrowski's routine frequently involved attending classes, doing the required course readings and case summaries, and then studying his growing library of national security texts which were increasingly becoming his primary interest and source of pleasure. He would typically find a footnote reference to a journal article while reading in the evening, and make a point of going the next day to the library between classes to find and photocopy the journal article. He would read the article the following evening and check the bibliography and footnotes for any references that would look interesting to follow up on. Over the months his shelves at home began to overflow with books and articles relating to history and national security.

In first year at law school Piotrowski attended a Saturday workshop on "Alternative Careers". Many of the speakers were people who graduated from law school and who used their knowledge of law and skills acquired in law school to pursue careers outside of the standard practice of law. Piotrowski remembered one lively and inspiring speaker who got into the broadcasting business. One of his tips was *"Figure out what you want to do, and then research the hell out of it!"* His message was that the more you know about a particular industry and business, the better you will be equipped to take advantage of opportunities to succeed in that field. Piotrowski took that message to heart. Unfortunately, his interest and knowledge of security and intelligence issues would subsequently be viewed with suspicion by some CSIS analysts. A number of them would write memos describing the research Piotrowski conducted as an obsession and imply that it was a malady. Piotrowski would subsequently wish the speaker had added the warning that the general principle does not apply to CSIS where knowing too much about CSIS and Canadian national security issues is a red flag.

In his second year at law school a visiting professor from abroad offered a course on national security law. Unfortunately, as was the case with most foreign visiting scholars, this professor was learning the subject matter as he was teaching the course, and it showed. Piotrowski wrote a paper for the course on security service accountability. Piotrowski did not have to use the library to write the paper. He had all the materials he needed at home including relevant government reports, bills, statutes, books, journal articles, copies of cases, etc. Piotrowski got an "A" on the paper and as the final course mark.

In May 1987 the law school sponsored a two-day conference relating to national security law. Piotrowski was thrilled to be able to attend the lectures and panel discussions as the topics. Some of the speakers and members of the audience were distinguished academics, journalists, lawyers, members of the national security establishment, and writers of some of the books in his library at home. Where else could a student mingle with the CSIS Director (Ted Finn showed up to deliver a keynote address after a cocktail reception and formal dinner) and Deputy Director, the Commissioner of the RCMP, and members of SIRC?

One of the scheduled speakers was a CBC news producer by the name of Jim Littleton. Littleton had written and hosted a series of radio documentaries titled *Dissent and Subversion* for the *Ideas* program of CBC Radio in 1983 during the controversy over Bill C-157. Piotrowski contacted the CBC and purchased a copy of the transcripts of the four-hours long documentary (it aired in four hour-long installments). Littleton also had a book published titled *Target Nation*. Piotrowski thought both of these products of his were poor and misguided. Nonetheless, he was looking forward to hearing Littleton speak to see what he might say. At the time Peter Wright's book *Spycatcher* (1987) was an international media sensation and Littleton made it the subject of his speech. One of the stories in *Spycatcher* was about a group of MI5 officers at one time who were unhappy about the nature and direction of the U.K. Government. They discussed among themselves what they could do about it, including some options that were beyond their mandate. During his speech Littleton used this episode from the book as an example of "subversion" and accused the security services themselves of being subversive and a threat to democracy. He stood on the stage and spoke in a condescending manner while looking down at three gentlemen sitting on the side in the audience. The three were senior CSIS officials, including a Deputy Director, Harry Brandes. The CSIS officials sat there expressionless.

After Littleton finished taking his shots at CSIS the moderator opened the floor up to questions from the audience. I took my copy of the transcripts of the Littleton "Dissent and Subversion" radio documentary and approached the microphone. I stated that I was surprised to hear Littleton speak of subversion and accuse the Security Services of being subversive, when he previously stated on CBC radio as part of a four-hour long documentary about the first CSIS Bill that he had come to the conclusion that subversion does not exist. I read the transcript and quoted the part where he discussed the threats that were identified in the Bill and stated categorically that he had come to the conclusion that "there is no such thing as subversion." So I asked him, how is it that three years ago you researched the topic enough to be able to produce a four-hour program categorically stating that there is no such thing as subversion and today you are insisting that subversion exists and is a threat? Which is it? Could it be that the question of whether or not subversion exists depends on the journalist's political agenda du jour?

There was an awkward silence after I finished asking this question. The situation became even more awkward and embarrassing as Littleton tried to wiggle out of the corner he had painted himself into by mumbling something about "that's not what I meant" and tried to distinguish the arguments he used in both occasions. He scrambled on his feet to find some sort of reasoning that might help save the day for him. Instead, the more he spoke, the more he seemed to find himself slowly squirming and sinking in quicksand. I actually started feeling sorry for Littleton as all eyes and ears in the auditorium were focused on him as he tried to extricate himself from this mess of his own creation. The moderator was sympathetic to Littleton's cause and saved him from drowning. The moderator came to Littleton's rescue and summarily cut him off while moving on to the next question from the floor. Later during the conference one of the law professors at Osgoode who specialized in ethics told me that he would have liked to see a debate between Littleton and me on the issue of dissent and subversion. I told him I would be happy to. Regrettably, it never happened.

The next day CSIS Deputy Director Harry Brandes went up to Piotrowski in the hallway outside the auditorium and congratulated Piotrowski on asking *"the best question of the conference"*. Brandes was an older gentleman and obviously an RCMP Security Service veteran. He smiled at Piotrowski in a friendly manner. They had a series of pleasant encounters and chats throughout the conference and Brandes gave Piotrowski his business card.

A year later the papers delivered at the conference were published in a book. Except Littleton's. Littleton and his presentation at the conference were not mentioned anywhere in the book.

In Piotrowski's last year at Osgoode he took an elective course in the political science department on the topic of intelligence that was taught by a professor who was a prolific critic of the western security and intelligence services. As part of the course requirements Piotrowski wrote a paper on the reform and future of CSIS. Piotrowski got an "A" from the professor for the paper and the course mark, but he wondered whether experts in the field might be able to provide him with any additional commentary that an academic couldn't. Piotrowski subsequently sent a copy of the paper to Harry Brandes and asked if he would be able to provide any feedback. Piotrowski's primary objective was to determine whether he "got it right" and whether his analysis was consistent with that of the Service.

In April 1988 Piotrowski received a letter from Brandes on the CSIS letterhead of his office. Brandes stated that he remembered meeting Piotrowski the previous year and *"...recall also being extremely impressed at the interventions and comments that you made at that time."* He congratulated Piotrowski on the paper and the *"wide ranging and well referenced scope of it"* and agreed with a number of his observations, although he added that *"you will understand that it is difficult for me to comment on a number of the overtly political judgments that you make but I encourage you to maintain interest in the Act and the Service. You may even wish to consider bringing your perceptives [sic] before the Parliamentary Committee which will be reviewing the Act late in 1989."* He added that he had *"taken the liberty of having someone else in our Service review your paper with a view to providing more specific comment."* He enclosed a copy of a recent report issued by the Solicitor General and a speech by the Director. Piotrowski was happy to receive Brandes' letter as it suggested that his general understanding of the issues in the realm of national security was consistent and not at odds with that of the management at CSIS. Piotrowski never received any feedback from whoever the "someone else" was.

The Deputy Director's use of the word "perceptives" caused Piotrowski to wonder. What did he mean? Perceptive is an adjective. Piotrowski suspected Brandes meant to write "perspectives". Did the Deputy Director not have an assistant to review documents for the Deputy Director's signature?

When the *CSIS Act* was passed in 1985 it contained a clause that required Parliament to review the Act after five years. A review committee was expected to be established in 1989. Although Piotrowski had not previously considered making a submission to the Parliamentary Committee, the fact that the Deputy Director at CSIS had encouraged Piotrowski to do so now made him reflect on the possibility.

Piotrowski also sent a copy of his paper on the reform and future of CSIS to Bob Kaplan, a Toronto area MP who was the former Solicitor General responsible for the passage of the *CSIS Act* and the creation of CSIS. To Piotrowski's delight, Kaplan called him a few weeks later and said that he appreciated Piotrowski sending him the paper. Kaplan had read it and discussed some of the points with Piotrowski. Kaplan was clearly proud of his legacy and happy to talk about the passage of the Act. Piotrowski was thrilled to be able to speak with the person who had been at the top of the political decision-making hierarchy with respect to the reform and creation of CSIS. One often learns some interesting historical anecdotes in conversations with key players that one won't find in any books.

At the time Piotrowski also became interested in the activities of a number of institutes, think tanks and associations that dealt with issues relating to National Security. One of them was the Canadian Association for Security and Intelligence Studies (CASIS). At one of their meetings Piotrowski met former RCMP Security Service Director John Starnes. Piotrowski subsequently sent him a copy of his paper on the Reform and Future of CSIS and asked him if he would have any comments that he was willing to share. Starnes replied with an informative letter in which he took issue with the suggestion in Piotrowski's paper that there appeared to be an intelligence failure during the October Crisis of 1970. Piotrowski learned a few things from Starnes' response and appreciated the feedback.

The International Security Institute (ISI) was an organization in Toronto that was headed by a former French General Antoine de Fougerolles. Piotrowski had previously heard de Fougerolles speak at one conference about the Cold War. De Fougerolles' presentation at the conference was about Soviet "active measures" and techniques used in disinformation campaigns. His presentation was the best Piotrowski had ever heard on the topic. After de Fougerolles' presentation, Piotrowski introduced himself and asked to be added to the Institute's mailing list so he would obtain copies of future newsletters and publications. Piotrowski kept in touch with de Fougerolles and enjoyed hearing him provide his analysis of historic and current events. Piotrowski particularly appreciated de Fougerolles' recommendations for further reading.

The ISI organized a conference in 1988 titled *Subversion in the 1980s: Myth or Reality?* De Fougerolles contacted Piotrowski and offered him an opportunity to present a paper at the conference. Piotrowski then researched and wrote a paper titled *Subversion and the Law in Canada* which he presented at the conference. Piotrowski was thrilled to be given the opportunity to participate and his paper was well-received. Other speakers included Zdzislaw M. Rurasz, the former Polish Ambassador to Japan who defected to the West after the imposition of martial law in Poland, as well as American Professor Guenter Lewy, who had just written a noteworthy article published in *Orbis* titled *Does America Need a Verfassungschutzbericht?* (Fall 1987). He also met Dave Thompson, a former RCMP and CSIS officer who was a veteran of the RCMP Security Service's counter-subversion section. Thompson approached Piotrowski after his presentation and congratulated him on his presentation. They exchanged contact information and kept in touch. Thompson would subsequently move to Ottawa and work in the management of security on Parliament Hill. About two years later Thompson called

Piotrowski and indicated that there was an employment opportunity in his Parliament Hill security offices. Thompson told Piotrowski that he would like to "bring him in", but Piotrowski declined as he had just accepted another more promising position.

Another person that Piotrowski had previously met and who was also at the conference was Col. Liam McNabb. McNabb was the head of the Institute of Strategic Studies (ISS), another think tank that Piotrowski had already become a member of and was on their mailing list. He had already acquired a number of their publications and was happy to receive their newsletters and conference publications.

After receiving the letter from Harry Brandes suggesting that Piotrowski bring his perspectives to the attention of the Parliamentary Committee that was going to review the *CSIS Act* in 1989, Piotrowski contacted the ISI and proposed to de Fougerolles that Piotrowski write a paper for publication in the ISI's journal on the reform of CSIS and discuss what should be done with the *CSIS Act*. De Fougerolles agreed and Piotrowski proceeded to get to work on drafting the article.

Piotrowski enjoyed and had learned a great deal through his attendance and participation in these conferences and exchanges with former and current senior management at CSIS (and the RCMP) and the former Minister. Piotrowski thought that CSIS might have interviewed those who were familiar with his participation and had interactions with him, but there was not a word about any interview with Brandes, Thompson, De Fougerolles, Piotrowski's law professors, McNabb or even Starnes in the file. Instead, some people who worked on Piotrowski's application file described his interests and activities as an unhealthy obsession.

In his research on KGB disinformation Piotrowski came across a number of books produced by a Soviet defector by the name of Yuri Bezmenov. Bezmenov had been a Novosti journalist who defected to Canada and one of his books was titled *No Novosti is Good News*. He claimed to have been a "co-opted" KGB agent who found the Soviet system reprehensible and defected while working abroad. Piotrowski managed to contact Bezmenov at one point when Bezmenov was living in Montreal. On one weekend trip to Montreal Piotrowski visited Bezmenov at his home and listened as Bezmenov elaborated on Soviet techniques of disinformation.

During the summers of 1986 and 1987 Piotrowski worked as a law student assistant in a small law office of two sole practitioners who shared office space. The pay was low, but he was primarily there for the learning opportunity. He worked on real estate and some civil court cases. It was a great learning experience and Piotrowski got along well with everyone who worked there.

While working at the law office Piotrowski enjoyed every opportunity to learn from the lawyers about legal issues and the practicalities relating to the establishment and maintenance of a law practice. One day while travelling with one of the lawyers from the office to a court building the lawyer told Piotrowski about how the sole practitioners came together to establish their law office. Piotrowski was told that the two sole practitioners decided to hire an associate to work for both of them and they ended up interviewing six candidates who were junior lawyers just starting their careers. Two of the candidates looked promising. The lawyer said that the two candidates seemed to be of equal strength and picking one was a challenge. However, one of the candidates sent the two interviewing lawyers a simple "Thank You" card. The lawyer said that the card made a positive impression. That candidate was offered the position. The mailing of the card was not a determining factor that resulted in the offer of employment, but it was something that the interviewers appreciated and considered a nice touch. Piotrowski made a mental note of the story and thought that in the future he might also develop a habit of sending such "Thank You" cards in similar circumstances. Unfortunately, Piotrowski would subsequently find out the hard way that such simple acts of professional courtesy can be regarded at CSIS as "unusual" and interpreted as symptoms of "forcefulness" which were treated as red flags.

After law school, Piotrowski's legal education would require him to complete a year of "articling" (internship) in a law office, and then complete the Bar Admission Course and exams. The two lawyers that

Piotrowski worked for during the summers offered Piotrowski a chance to article with their offices after graduation from law school, but Piotrowski wanted to seek experience in a larger firm.

Piotrowski secured an articling position at a medium size law firm in North York that specialized in real estate law and had several related divisions, including corporate/commercial, litigation, and family law. The firm had an articling program that provided students with rotation opportunities. His annual pay was $27,000 (about the starting salary of a CSIS Intelligence Officer at the time). There were four articling students at the firm and they shared a large office. The other students had studied in Edmonton, Winnipeg and Windsor. Piotrowski tried to be helpful to the others with assistance in research and getting a grip on new issues when they were given files on topics about which they may not have been familiar. Despite the competition between them, Piotrowski understood the frustration that all students occasionally felt and was willing to help. Whenever the students rotated from one area to another, they had to hand off their ongoing files to the next student who would take over the file. Piotrowski always wrote detailed memos to the files with all the relevant background information, status, and next steps so the next person on the file could hit the ground running. The one female student among the others told Piotrowski how much she appreciated that. Piotrowski made his law books available to the others. He did not mind lending them if they could be of use. Unfortunately, the other students did not reciprocate. Notwithstanding this year-long record, some CSIS investigators would falsely state in Piotrowski's file that he was not a "team player".

There was a federal election during the Fall of 1988. It turned out that the partners of the law firm where Piotrowski worked were Liberal Party supporters and they offered the use of their offices and telephones after normal business hours to the Bob Kaplan re-election campaign team for purposes of contacting constituents and drumming up support. Piotrowski volunteered to join them. Piotrowski had previously volunteered to do some door-to-door canvassing during the 1987 provincial election for a Progressive

Conservative incumbent MPP by the name of Yuri Shymko (he lost). Piotrowski was happy to contribute to Kaplan's campaign (he won). In both cases it was primarily the candidate that Piotrowski was supporting. Participating in the campaigns was a tremendous education in that element of the political process and an exciting opportunity. Piotrowski worked on the phone banks and other assigned tasks. However, the most exciting part of the campaigns was door-to-door canvassing with the candidate.

The last time Piotrowski saw Kaplan in Toronto Piotrowski told him that he was planning to move to Ottawa to complete the Bar Admission Course. Kaplan told Piotrowski that he should contact him once he'd settled in Ottawa. Piotrowski appreciated Kaplan's willingness to keep in touch with him.

Over the three-year period at law school Piotrowski's thoughts about future career options underwent an evolution and occasionally changed. He often thought of being a civil litigator, or a corporate/commercial lawyer, or possibly pursuing a doctorate and becoming a professor. However, he also increasingly thought about applying to CSIS a second time. Piotrowski had developed a degree of understanding about the Cold War conflict between East and West and wanted to contribute to the defence of the West and the protection of the freedoms that we enjoyed. Since Piotrowski's previous failed application in 1985 he had come a long way in his education and believed that he could be an asset to the organization. He also thought it would be a natural extension of all the studying that he had done which was of sincere and genuine interest to him.

When Piotrowski started his articling year in the summer of 1988, he decided to submit an application to CSIS for a position as an Intelligence Officer. Law was interesting, but by this time it was not his primary interest or passion. He planned to complete his articling year and the subsequent Bar Admission Course and exams to obtain his license to practice, but he increasingly thought that what would like to do is devote his career to the defence of Canada's national security. He had read somewhere that FBI applicants had to be law graduates. CSIS was looking for university grads and might appreciate some recruits with legal backgrounds. By the time Piotrowski finished the bar exams he thought he might have more education than the majority of CSIS applicants and would a good chance of being seriously considered. Piotrowski drafted a two-page cover letter and updated his resume. In his application he included transcripts of his law school marks and those from McGill as well as a few "To Whom it May Concern" letters of reference from previous employers. He also included a copy of his paper on the reform of CSIS and the history of subversion and the law in Canada. He mailed the bulging envelope to the CSIS recruiting mailing address which was a post office box in Ottawa and crossed his fingers.

Piotrowski subsequently found out that McNabb of the Institute of Strategic Studies was a lecturer at the Sir William Stephenson Academy for new CSIS recruits at Camp Borden. As CSIS obviously valued McNabb's expertise, Piotrowski subsequently asked McNabb if he would write a letter of reference to CSIS regarding Piotrowski and his conference presentation on subversion. McNabb asked Piotrowski for his resume and then discussed it with him over the phone and said he would send in a letter of reference. Piotrowski never heard about it after and did not see any reference to it or copy in his application file.

A few months after sending in his application Piotrowski received a call from someone at CSIS asking him to come to the CSIS regional office in Toronto for an interview. Piotrowski was ecstatic after hanging up the phone.

I remember getting that phone call and being so happy. I believed I had a realistic idea of what CSIS did and what national security was about. I believed that the intelligence officers at CSIS were good people doing important work. I felt I could contribute. I was willing to devote my career to the organization and its mission. I felt confident that I had a good chance to successfully pass the recruit screening stages. How wrong I was! It would take a couple of years before I discovered how I had misjudged CSIS and its personnel. In hindsight, I knew little. Regrettably, CSIS knew even less.

CHAPTER 2:
FIRST INTERVIEW

On January 12, 1989, Krzysztof Piotrowski arranged to take time off work and went to the Toronto offices of CSIS for an interview. The CSIS officers were located downtown in a building near the base of the CN Tower. The offices looked modern. Piotrowski met a CSIS officer named David Onions. He looked like he was around forty years old. He was of average height and slim. Onions invited Piotrowski into his office. Onions gave the impression that he had been in the role of being the first to meet new candidates for a while and would follow a standard choreographed routine. His demeanour was of an experienced police officer who had been assigned to a desk job and was trying to be as professional about it as he could be. However, while giving his memorized blurb about CSIS and the recruiting process one could tell that he was bored and just "doing his job".

This first interview in the recruiting process was referred to as a "personal suitability" interview. It served to provide CSIS with an opportunity to make preliminary assessments of candidates and to screen out those who were truly non-starters.

Onions began by telling Piotrowski a little about CSIS and the first steps in the recruitment process. If Piotrowski "passed" this interview he would be invited to a series of written tests. If he passed those he would be invited for more interviews.

Onions then asked Piotrowski a lengthy series of questions about his background, family, education, studies, current activities, and hobbies. Onion also asked Piotrowski about his political views and any related activity, his knowledge of national security issues, what Piotrowski knew about CSIS and its mandate, and what he thought the job would involve, etc.

Piotrowski took the meeting seriously. He tried to project the appearance of a candidate who was knowledgeable, serious, and sincerely interested in becoming an Intelligence Officer at CSIS. Piotrowski wanted Onions to know that he was a candidate who understood the seriousness of national security and what was at stake. He provided Onions with detailed and relevant answers to all of Onions' questions as he took notes. On several occasions Onions told him to slow down and repeat some things. Onions gave the impression that he previously encountered short "yes" or "no" answers from previous recruits and was not used to details and taking so many notes. Piotrowski got the impression that the more he talked and the more Onions took notes, the better. Regrettably, that was a false interpretation that Piotrowski would later regret.

Piotrowski told Onions about his experiences visiting Poland and what he understood to be the differences between communist societies and liberal democracies. He told him that he considered himself a middle-of-the-road centrist or slightly right of centre liberal democrat who appreciated the wealth that capitalism and the free markets could create and the role of the state in some redistribution to ensure that all citizens had access to education, health care, and a social safety net.

Piotrowski believed that the only legitimate Government was one with a mandate from the people, and that could only be conveyed through free elections. One of the corresponding challenges for liberal democracy concerned would be the participation in such elections of those who were intent on destroying such democratic institutions if they came to power.

Concerning economics, Piotrowski told Onions that he believed in the free market system. He also noted what the Soviets had now been admitting since Gorbachev's "perestroika" and "glasnost" policies had triggered a new openness in the USSR, namely, that communism is a bankrupt system. Of course, the abuses of an unrestricted market economy have to be restrained and Piotrowski indicated his support for legislation protecting labour such as the right to form unions as well as minimum wage and maximum hours of work type of legislation. He also supported competition type of legislation to prevent corporate abuse of dominant positions in the marketplace and monopolies (anti-trust).

Piotrowski did not find any of his questions to be difficult or a cause of any discomfort. He was happy to speak about his perspectives with someone whom he thought would share similar views and presumably appreciate them.

Piotrowski brought and showed Onions some samples of his university writing as well as his letter-to-the-editor that was published in the *Montreal Gazette*.

During the interview Piotrowski told him that he was in the process of writing a paper for publication about CSIS on the occasion of the five-year review of the *CSIS Act*, but would not pursue it if it would jeopardize his application. Onions told Piotrowski that that was not a problem and that Piotrowski should go ahead. Onions said that the Service has often hired high profile people. Onions said that the only restriction was that Piotrowski should not reveal that he is an applicant to the Service. Piotrowski was happy to hear that. Unfortunately, Piotrowski would later discover that what Onions told him was not true. He would later regret that Onions had not warned Piotrowski that such publications were in fact a problem for CSIS.

Piotrowski raised another question. He indicated that he was completing his articling year with a law firm in Toronto but was increasingly thinking of moving to Ottawa to complete the Bar Admission course and exams. He hoped that he would be able to join CSIS after being "called to the Bar", and would already be in Ottawa and able to start working at CSIS headquarters. However, if that did not work out, Piotrowski increasingly thought of a career in government and public policy if his CSIS aspirations did not materialize. He asked Onions if Piotrowski's plans for moving from Toronto would cause any complication in his application process. Onions told him that was not a problem and should keep CSIS informed about his move and future contact information. Piotrowski was happy to hear that.

At the end of the interview Onions then did something Piotrowski would never forget.

After three uninterrupted hours our meeting came to an end. Onions shrugged his shoulders as if he was exhausted and said to me "You're head and shoulders above all the other candidates". Onions said it with an air of resignation as though his job was to find and identify the grounds upon which to disqualify as many candidates as possible and had failed in this case and was defeated. Imagine how I felt! It seemed that all the things I had learned over the years and all the positions I held and expressed during the interview were not only relevant and appropriate, but consistent with CSIS culture. At least, that's what I thought. Unfortunately, that euphoria that I felt at that time was to prove baseless. CSIS does not care if you are head and shoulders above all the other candidates. CSIS considers anything unusual to be suspicious, and that's a red flag.

Onions told Piotrowski about the next steps, one of which involved French language tests. Piotrowski asked about the format and content so he could prepare. Coincidentally, across the hall from Onions' office was a small meeting room in which a French language teacher had just finished a class with a CSIS staff member. The door was open and Onions introduced Piotrowski and the teacher, Suzanne Guibault, to each other. Onions asked if she could tell Piotrowski something about the language test and what Piotrowski could expect. Onions then excused himself and stepped out for a few moments. Guibault was a middle-age woman who smiled pleasantly and Piotrowski started speaking with her in French. Guibault immediately recognized that Piotrowski's command of French basics was good, however, Piotrowski explained that it had been years since he wrote anything in French and he had forgotten much of the rules of grammar and some vocabulary. Guibault explained that the standard government exams involved tests in written French, reading comprehension and oral communication. Piotrowski indicated that he was confident he could pass, but very much needed some practice to brush up and prepare. Piotrowski asked her if she knew anyone who could help coach him and help prepare for the exams, and she offered to do so. They exchanged contact information and Piotrowski indicated he would follow up. Onions then returned and escorted Piotrowski to the front door.

Keeping in mind the tip that his former employer shared with him, Piotrowski sent Onions a "Thank You" card thanking him for the meeting. Piotrowski then waited for the next call from CSIS. In the meantime, he started to brush up on his French.

With Onion's giving Piotrowski the "go ahead" for the publication of his paper on the review of the *CSIS Act* he reinvigorated his working on it after office hours and eventually submitted a final draft to de Fougerolles for publication in a subsequent issue of the Institute's quarterly Journal. He titled the paper *"The Reform of the CSIS Act – How far Should it Go?"* The article's thesis was that the *CSIS Act* adequately balanced the interests of national security and civil liberties and did not require any major adjustment at that time. Piotrowski suspected that academics, left wing and civil liberties groups would advocate for a reduction of the powers of the Service along with greater "oversight" and red tape. Piotrowski's stance was to take a middle-of-the-road approach and propose the maintenance of the status quo. Piotrowski looked forward to seeing the final product in print as it would offer a contrast to much of the growing criticism of CSIS in the context of the five-year review of the Act.

CHAPTER 3:
TESTS AND MORE TESTS

A few days after his meeting with Onions, Piotrowski called Guibault to set up a meeting as part of his preparation for the French tests. He knew the French language test date would be set soon and he did not have any time to waste. Guilbault invited Piotrowski to her home which was a small apartment and looked like a temporary location for her. She had some French reference texts that she was willing to lend Piotrowski. She was also willing to spend some time with him to refresh his knowledge of French grammar and practice his French speaking skills. Piotrowski had not spoken French since leaving Montreal since most of his former classmates and workmates were not fluent in French and he appreciated Guibault's willingness to help him prepare for the language tests. Piotrowski visited Guilbault on two occasions and each time gave her a bottle of wine as a gift to thank her for her time and kindness.

At first Piotrowski was unsure of the nature of Guibault's relationship with CSIS. He hoped that she was a permanent staff member and would thus effectively be a conduit through which CSIS would be able to obtain another assessment of him as a candidate. Guibault informed him that she was a language teacher who had a series of short-term contracts with CSIS to teach their staff. She told Piotrowski that she had been married and was for years a mother and a housewife. However, she had been unhappy and once her kids reached adulthood, she got a divorce and turned to teaching French as her path to independence and her second life as a liberated woman. Guibault smiled a lot and was very pleasant, but Piotrowski detected that under the veneer she was still unhappy. It turned out that her relationship with her boyfriend with whom she had been living in Ottawa had soured and that appeared to be the reason why she embarked on a hiatus to Toronto. She indicated that her current contract was set to expire shortly and she was preparing to return to Ottawa. Piotrowski told her that he was in the process of completing his articling year at one law firm and was planning to move to Ottawa to complete the Bar Admission Course and exams, following which he hoped to join CSIS. They agreed to keep in touch and reconnect in Ottawa.

A couple of weeks later Piotrowski was contacted by CSIS and asked to attend their offices for the French language tests. Piotrowski arranged to take the morning off from work under the guise of a medical appointment. A number of candidates were writing the tests at the same time, but the circumstances did not allow the candidates to mingle and chat. Piotrowski wondered who they were and what their backgrounds were, but everyone remained silent while waiting and disappeared after the tests were over. The standard government language test constituted a series of separate multiple-choice tests for reading comprehension and the written language. These were easy to mark and the candidate had to get a certain percentage of correct answers above a minimum threshold to pass. There was also a short writing test requiring one to write about a page in French on any topic, followed by a brief oral exam with an examiner. A failure in any of these tests at this stage resulted in the immediate rejection of one's candidacy. After the tests Piotrowski saw Guilbault in one of the classrooms across the hall and proceeded to chat with her before leaving. He said the tests went well and he felt confident. Shortly afterward Onions appeared and told Piotrowski that the multiple-choice tests had been marked and Piotrowski had successfully passed them. Onions mentioned that two of the other candidates had failed and dismissively stated that they were "out". Piotrowski was told that the writing and oral tests were being assessed. If he passed them, he could expect to receive a phone call inviting him to the next round of tests.

Once again, I left the CSIS office feeling great. I was so grateful to my parents for having sent me to a French school when I was a kid. However, in hindsight, I wish I had failed that language exam. It would have put an end to the ordeal and would have saved me a lot of subsequent grief and regret.

The next day Piotrowski received a phone call and was invited to the CSIS offices the following week for a series of tests that would take the entire morning. The first test involved an English comprehension and writing test. Piotrowski was given a text of about 10 pages and given 90 minutes to write a summary. It was easy. The passage was from one of the McDonald Commission studies written by Professor Franks. Piotrowski had the McDonald Commission reports and all the related studies at home. He had thoroughly studied them and was very familiar with them. Piotrowski recognized the passage they gave him to write a summary of. The test was meant to assess his ability to understand the text and explain it in a succinct manner. Piotrowski's writing case summaries on a daily basis in law school was similar to doing this kind of exercise. No sweat.

After a brief break, the second test that Piotrowski was required to take was the Management "In-Basket" test. The test involved going through a pile of documents ranging from memos and messages to reports and determining how to deal with each one. It also involved writing clear explanations for the examiners and memos that one would have to prepare with instructions and requests for employees and co-workers. The challenge was primarily two-fold: one was the volume of tasks and the time restriction, and the other was the trick questions. For example, one memo on top of the pile would prompt a certain time of course of action, and then at the bottom of the pile there would be an updated memo describing how the circumstances had completely changed since the date of the last memo forcing one to cross out any previously written obsolete response and write out a new one (before the allotted time expired). Piotrowski found the test a pleasant challenge. His experience working in law offices helped assess the situations and drafting the memos describing the appropriate course of action.

Finally, Piotrowski was also required to write some psychological tests. These involved a series of "true of false" and multiple-choice questions.

After the tests were over Piotrowski emerged from the CSIS offices feeling that his application to CSIS was on track and the recruitment process had not tripped him up or raised any obstacles. At least, none that he was aware of. Before leaving the CSIS offices Piotrowski was given a series of forms to fill out for purposes of obtaining the necessary security clearance. Government security clearances come with different categories and levels. As an Intelligence Officer he would need a "Top Secret" security clearance. The forms and details that he had to provide about his background were extensive (e.g., all the addresses where he lived for the past decade, where he studied, worked, lists of references who had known him for at least 10 years, etc.) If he had lived in just one place and studied at just one school and had just one job, filling out the forms would have been a breeze. It wasn't. Piotrowski filled out the forms and hand-delivered them back to the CSIS offices.

Piotrowski later found out that he had made a mistake with one previous address number that he provided. Years earlier in Calgary he had briefly lived with his mother in an apartment in a building with the street address number of 1038. However, Piotrowski mistakenly wrote 138. It was an honest error. Regrettably, Piotrowski later found out that the CSIS officer investigating Piotrowski's background in Calgary highlighted the problem in the application file as if he had uncovered a nefarious CSIS infiltration scheme. This was compounded by the fact that the CSIS investigator could not find any reference to Piotrowski in the city telephone book for the years that he lived in Calgary. It did not occur to CSIS that the home phone was listed in the city directory under his mother's name, Maria Adamska.

Piotrowski waited for the next call from CSIS and what he hoped would be an invitation to proceed to the next stage in the recruitment process.

CHAPTER 4:
MEETING WITH
INTERNAL SECURITY

In April of 1989 Piotrowski received a phone call from a CSIS officer named Julia Goodale. She called Piotrowski at work and asked to schedule an appointment for him to come to the CSIS offices for a meeting with her. She was from the internal security division and the meeting constituted the next step in the application process.

Piotrowski told her that he had already taken several hours off work on different days to attend these meetings and write the tests. It was getting a little awkward at the office as he could not tell his employer that he was going to CSIS offices and each time he had to tell a fictitious story about one medical appointment after another. Piotrowski asked if he could meet with her in the evening or on a weekend. Goodale told Piotrowski she was doing some painting at her home that weekend but would be able to meet him at the CSIS offices on Sunday at 7 p.m. Piotrowski thanked her for her flexibility in this matter.

The following Sunday Piotrowski drove downtown and parked a few blocks away in an empty parking lot and went over to the CSIS offices. The offices were largely empty except for one lonely security guard. Piotrowski was struck by Goodale's appearance. She was in her early to mid-thirties. Goodale was slim and had shoulder-length brown hair with chiseled facial features. She was physically quite attractive. She also gave the appearance of being very intelligent. "Why couldn't all the brainy young women in law school look like this?" Piotrowski wondered. He would later discover that his first impression of Goodale was a false one and he had completely misjudged her.

Goodale led Piotrowski through the largely empty and dark corridors to a bare office where she sat behind a desk and told Piotrowski to take the seat in front of the desk. She offered him a glass of water and gave him a brief introduction. She said that she was from the internal security division and she wanted to speak with him about himself and his background. She told him that she wanted Piotrowski to "talk" as she crossed her arms across her chest. As she said this her body language suggested a presumptive adoption of skepticism and a challenge to convince her otherwise. She had a clipboard with paper and pen nearby and made it obvious that she was going to take notes. Piotrowski welcomed the challenge.

She then proceeded to give Piotrowski some general topics and asked him to talk about them. It quickly became obvious that she wanted to cover the broad range of all potential areas where Piotrowski might have some character weaknesses that may leave him subject to blackmail or may provoke him to do something stupid. She was interested in anything that would raise concerns about the extent to which they could trust him.

Did Piotrowski drink? No. He'd been drunk before from excessively drinking at parties in his teens, but never really liked the taste of alcoholic beverages. He occasionally had a beer. It might be with a meal with other people, but he rarely had more than one on such occasions. If someone left a six-pack at his home it might stay in the fridge for weeks.

Drugs. Like most teens who try to explore and experiment with adventure and excitement, Piotrowski had tried cannabis in high school. He had not smoked it in years. He did not like buying drugs on the black market and did not hang around with people who did. He also thought the cost was excessive and a waste of money.

Sexual behaviour. Piotrowski told Goodale that he "was a heterosexual and proud of it" with a deadpan delivery. At that point, Goodale burst into laughter. However, it was not just a chuckle but such a deep belly laugh that she had to put her clipboard down and hold her stomach for a few moments until she regained her composure. Piotrowski thought that her laughter eased whatever tension existed and was a good sign. Goodale was clearly enjoying herself and effectively encouraged Piotrowski to carry on. Piotrowski went on to tell her that he had attended boys' schools in his teens and did not meet many girls at that time but had his fair share of girlfriends since then. He would not be potentially subject to blackmail for engaging in any form of "alternative" or "perverse" sexual activity.

Finances. Piotrowski told her about my history of part-time jobs in high school and working at the Banff Springs Hotel in the summer of 1981. He told her about his practice of banking his paycheques and living off his tips while other guys were usually broke within three days after payday. She laughed at that. Piotrowski told her that he has saved up $2,500 that summer. He told her about his investments in high interest GICs in the early 1980s and how his parents paid for his school and did not charge him anything for room and board because they valued education and were willing to support him while he was in school. Piotrowski told her about his purchasing a condo with his girlfriend using the money he had saved up by then and that his father contributed the remainder of his share. He told her about his summer jobs in the law office in Toronto. He told her about breaking up with his girlfriend and buying out her share of the condo, taking a mortgage to finance it, and renting out two rooms to students. He told her the cost of the home, his share which he contributed, the size of the mortgage that he took out to buy her share and what the home was currently valued at. That was his financial story. He was lucky to have parental financial support when he needed it. He was happy to have had work experience which generated income. He was proud that he was disciplined with his savings was able to invest in GICs when the interest rates were high. Piotrowski had not studied the stock market and had no experience with stock picking. He did not have any risky investments.

She then asked Piotrowski about his political views and activities. The discussion of this topic took up the longest stretch during the interview. Piotrowski repeated all the things that he had told Onions, and went into more detail. He told her about his family background coming from Poland and having been victims of communist oppression. He mentioned his grandfather being murdered by the Soviet NKVD in the Katyn Massacre, and that his parents managed to leave Poland on separate scholarships at a time when even though Stalin was dead, Poland was still a Stalinist country. He mentioned to her that his father was an anti-communist and he did not appreciate his father's perspective were until he had the experience of visiting Poland on three occasions in the mid-1970s and had the joy of standing in daily bread lines.

I told her that when I had visited Poland, I found watching the television news fascinating because of its contrast with that in the West and the blatant propaganda. I gave her some examples. Typical newscasts would begin with celebrations of joint "Poland-USSR potato growing treaty", or coal mining treaty, or some other joint venture. Interviews would be done with the most unenthusiastic workers and farmers talking about how they were meeting their production quotas. Then they would talk about international news and announce that the Communist Part of the USA had its annual convention in some dingy hotel basement in a New York City slum somewhere. That was the kind of thing one that one never saw on TV back home. When was the last time the CBC covered a Canadian Communist Party convention?

As I told Goodale these stories and anecdotes that were part of my political education, she would repeatedly burst out laughing. Occasionally it bordered on hysterical laughter. It was obvious that she had never heard these issues discussed, and certainly not in this way, and that she was enjoying the discourse. Her laughter was contagious and made me laugh as well. It also encouraged me to keep up with the delivery.

I then described some of the literature that I read. I told her about some of my favourite books and those from which I had learned a lot. With respect to books that exposed the fraud of communist ideology and the myth of an egalitarian society, I pointed out to her that most people are aware of George Orwell's Animal Farm that was published in 1945. However, how many people, including political science students, had read Milovan Djilas' The New Class: An Analysis of the Communist System which was published in 1957, or Michael Voslensky's Nomenklatura: The Soviet Ruling Class which was published in 1984? Those books are masterpieces in their description of how the Communist Party and its leaders effectively rule by dictatorship and reserve the privileges for themselves. Goodale nodded and kept taking notes. From her facial expression I thought she was familiar with the books.

I then shared with her my thoughts about two other books that I enjoyed reading and contemplating, Arkady Shevchenko's Breaking with Moscow and Romuald Spasowski's The Liberation of One. I asked her if she was familiar with these books and she nodded affirmatively as she scribbled her notes. The more she wrote and nodded at me approvingly, the more I felt encouraged to keep talking. I discussed the two books and the lives of their authors. Shevchenko's book was a fascinating story of a careerist within the Soviet Ministry of Foreign Affairs and who eventually rose to become the Under Secretary General of the U.N. in New York. Eventually he became so disillusioned with the Soviet attitude and behaviour that he sought to defect. The CIA convinced him to stay in place and supply them for intelligence for a while. Eventually he felt the heat of KGB surveillance and when he was instructed to return to Moscow for consultations, he became the highest-ranking Soviet official to defect.

In contrast, Romuald Spasowski's book is one of a Pole who was initially an ardent believer in communist ideology. He joined the Communist regime early in his life and rose in the diplomatic corps to be the Polish Ambassador to multiple countries. Like Shevchenko, he too became disillusioned with the Communist regime. At the time that martial law was declared in Poland to *squash the Solidarity trade union Spasowski was Poland's Ambassador to the U.S. He defected and wrote his memoirs.*

I told Goodale how I enjoyed reading both books that were so well-written and historically informative. She kept nodding approvingly while taking notes. It was thrilling to be able to talk about these books with someone who appeared to know the stories, understand their significance and appreciate them as much as I did.

After about an hour and a half, Goodale suggested they take a break and go to the staff lounge where there was a kettle and make some coffee. There was still more to discuss and it was going to be a long evening.

After the short break Piotrowski continued by telling Goodale about his undergraduate and law school experiences. Piotrowski told her about how he wrote an essay in a university student paper criticizing the unilateral disarmament that the peace movement was promoting. He told her about the rebuttal from a left-wing critic who suggested that only those with posters of McCarthy on their walls would take Piotrowski seriously. Goodale burst out laughing again. Piotrowski joined her in the laughter and pointed out what he thought she was already aware of, namely that the nature of political activism on university campuses was often left-wing and that anyone who voiced support for Reagan's foreign policies with respect to NATO and the Soviet Union was bound to be denounced in the student newspapers by the hardcore leftist activists as a McCarthyist and a fascist. Goodale kept on laughing. Piotrowski told Goodale that the debate in the student newspaper went on for a few months and he enjoyed the intellectual challenge and learned a lot from the experience. However, he regretted it when opponents would resort to personal and demeaning attacks which would spoil the tone of the debate. Piotrowski prided himself on not crossing that line. However, Piotrowski pointed out that such name-calling should not be taken literally or seriously as it was more reflective of the accuser than the intended target.

Piotrowski told her that this bias was occasionally evident in the media. He then described how he read some blatant Soviet anti-American propaganda in the *Montreal Gazette* regarding nuclear negotiations and peace. He explained that he wrote a letter to the editor, which was published. However, Piotrowski pointed out that while he thought he had corrected the record, a week later the *Gazette* published a rebuttal from the Soviet writer and refused to publish Piotrowski's follow up response. Piotrowski stated that the editors gave the first and last word to a Soviet spokesman, and wondered when was the last time *Pravda* gave such privilege to the CIA or Radio Free Europe? Again, Goodale burst out laughing.

Piotrowski then described some of the classes that he had in university and some of the highlights of professorial stupidity, such as the professor who claimed that the government of the Soviet Union was "perfectly legitimate because there is no opposition", or the one who claimed that only a revolution and the abolishment of private property could resolve employer and employee disputes, or the criminal law professor who lectured that the greatest threat to our civil liberties was from the cops and CSIS, etc. Piotrowski elaborated on how he caught Jim Littleton contradicting himself on the issue of subversion at the law school conference.

To each of these anecdotes, Goodale would repeatedly burst into laughter. She seemed to have a healthy sense of humour and it was a refreshing experience for Piotrowski to be able to discuss these incidents with someone who appeared to appreciate the absurdity of the situations. The more she laughed however, the more Piotrowski felt compelled to continue in the same vein. They were both laughing and enjoying the discussion. Or so it seemed to Piotrowski at the time.

One of the last questions that Goodale asked Piotrowski was about who had he told about his application. He told her that he had informed his parents. His father had subsequently mentioned to Piotrowski that he had told one of his friends. Piotrowski told Goodale that he then repeated his request to his father to not mention it to anyone else as it was obviously supposed to be kept confidential.

He was confident that his father understood the importance of the matter and would not tell anyone else. Piotrowski also told Goodale that he had informed de Fougerolles as he sought the General's advice as well as McNabb whom he asked for a letter of reference.

Piotrowski left the CSIS offices after 11 p.m. It was a long interview. He was exhausted but pleasantly energized. He felt like he had connected with someone who was on the same wavelength. If there were other people like her at CSIS, and he was sure there were, then he thought he would probably fit right in. He would only find out later how he had completely misread the situation. Goodale's report on the meeting would cast suspicion on everything Piotrowski said and she would suggest that he might be a spy.

Piotrowski sent Goodale a "Thank You" card and thought that so far his application to CSIS appeared to be on track. His sending Goodale the card would turn out to be a bad move. Although Onions did not mention it in his report of his meeting with Piotrowski, Goodale referred to it in a negative light and characterized it as "unusual". Unaware of how he had inadvertently committed a *faux pas* which would be highlighted in his file and contribute to a perception that he was inappropriately "forceful", Piotrowski waited for the next call from CSIS. The next step in the process would involve the psychology interview.

Shortly after Piotrowski's interview with Goodale a new issue of the International Security Institute quarterly journal was published containing Piotrowski's article about the reform and future of the *CSIS Act*. He got a number of copies from de Fougerolles and was thrilled. In a 150-page issue his article was the leading one in the issue and took up 37 pages. Piotrowski sent a copy to the CSIS recruiting mail box address with a letter asking that it be added to his application.

De Fougerolles sent a few copies of the journal issue to CSIS Director Reid Morden and offered to forward more copies if requested. Morden subsequently sent de Fougerolles a letter requesting 15 copies of the issue containing Piotrowski's article. Years later Piotrowski would meet a former RCMP and CSIS veteran who left CSIS and became a security consultant and frequent media commentator on national security issues. When Piotrowski introduced himself the former CSIS officer said that he knew who Piotrowski was and appreciated his article when it was published. He told Piotrowski that he used it in the training of new CSIS recruits. Despite the "middle-of-the-road" thesis reflected in the article, the CSIS Director's interest in getting 15 copies for his organization and its use in teaching recruits, Piotrowski would later read in his CSIS application file repeated accusations by investigators and analysts that Piotrowski was an "extremist" who was unable to be objective and would likely engage in internal dissent and be a source of trouble and embarrassment for the Service.

CHAPTER 5:
THE PSYCHOLOGY DEBACLE

A few weeks following his meeting with Goodale Piotrowski was contacted and asked to visit the CSIS offices again for an interview with someone from the psychology unit at CSIS. Again, Piotrowski made some sort of arrangement to take time off work without anyone knowing where he was going or what for.

When Piotrowski arrived at the CSIS offices he was told to wait. A few moments later a short and thin man about 30 years old came to greet him and escort him to a small meeting room. He introduced himself as Vincent Gendron and indicated that he was a member of the CSIS psychology unit at headquarters in Ottawa. Piotrowski realized that Gendron had not just come to Toronto to interview him and was probably interviewing all the candidates who were still in the process. Piotrowski had already taken the written psychology test and assumed that Gendron was familiar with the results and the results of this interview were going to be used to draw up some sort of psychological profile.

The interview with Vincent Gendron was very strange. Gendron's behaviour was odd. He had an ice-cold appearance. His facial expression was devoid of any warm and human qualities. His posture and behaviour gave the impression that he was more of a robot than a normal human being. I also got the impression from appearance, grooming and mannerisms that there was something effeminate about him. I politely smiled and tried to be pleasant, but he did not reciprocate. Almost immediately I sensed that he did not like me. I don't know what prompted his subtle hostility towards me. I wondered if he would have been friendlier had I been French. I said a few words in French and tried to establish a warmer rapport with him, but it was futile. All I can say is that from the start I had this feeling that this guy was weird.

Gendron began by asking a series of straightforward questions about Piotrowski's background. Then he asked what are Piotrowski's hobbies and what did Piotrowski do in his spare time. This had already been asked of Piotrowski several times before with no apparently problem. But this time there was a difference. Piotrowski's hobbies included reading, researching and writing. In the past his writing had only been published in student newspapers (apart from the one letter to the *Montreal Gazette*). However, to this interview he was able to bring a copy of the recently published ISI journal with his article about the *CSIS Act*. On the basis that a "picture is worth a thousand words" Piotrowski took a copy of the journal article out of his briefcase and held it out to give to Gendron. Piotrowski thought that Gendron would take it from his hand and flip through it while Piotrowski elaborated on his hobbies. He was still feeling good about its publication a few weeks before. Unfortunately, Gendron did not budge. He neither reached out with one hand to take it from Piotrowski and flip through it nor did he tell Piotrowski that he did not want to see it. He did not even look at it. Instead, Gendron remained stiff as though he had a poker up his backside and showed no expression on his face while attempting to pierce Piotrowski with his stare.

I was very puzzled by Gendron's behaviour which struck me as surprisingly rude and unnecessary. What was the point of his ignoring the journal that I tried to hand over to him? He asked me what were my hobbies and I was telling him, but I also wanted to illustrate my answer by showing him an example that was hot off the press. He did not even look at it or acknowledge it. The way he sat frozen and stared at me with a fixed gaze made me feel like I was a monkey in a cage being observed by God knows who and for what? After a moment of awkward silence I tried to get on with the interview as smoothly as I could by putting the document down, answering his questions, and maintaining eye contact with him. I was not sure what he was trying to accomplish, but I did not want to give him the impression that he somehow intimidated or flustered me. Throughout the rest of the interview I kept my head up, maintained eye contact and provided short answers which were to the point. Unlike Goodale who encouraged me to "talk", this guy gave me the impression that he was not interested in details.

One of Gendron's subsequent questions was about Piotrowski's career ambitions. Piotrowski replied that he hoped to work as an Intelligence Officer and contribute to the work of CSIS. In the long run Piotrowski hoped over his career to be able to rise in the hierarchy through promotions as far as he could go. He thought that showing some interest in the role of senior management and confirming that he had some ambition would be a good thing. That was a big mistake. But Piotrowski would only find out about that later.

Gendron only smiled once at me when the interview was over and we shook hands goodbye. Of all the interviews and tests that I had during the application process, this was the only one that left me with an uncomfortable feeling. I could not figure out why that guy refused to reach out when I tried to show him a copy of my article and why he was so stiff. In all the years before and since that interview, I had never been in a situation with someone as odd and abnormal as this guy. Based on the sour feeling I had after this interview I decided not to send Gendron a "Thank You" card. That turned out to be a wise move as I subsequently discovered that his assessment of me was dismal and sending him a word of thanks would have made it worse.

Although this interview left Piotrowski with a bitter feeling, he was looking forward to the next steps in the recruitment process and his upcoming move to Ottawa.

CHAPTER 6:
MOVING TO OTTAWA

Piotrowski's year of articling with the law firm in Toronto was educational and memorable. Professionally, he acquired more knowledge and skills relating to the practice of law. On a personal level, in the early part of the year he dated a young lady whom he met in the elevator who worked for another office on a separate floor in the building. However, in the second half of the year he became involved in a romantic relationship with one of the legal secretaries at the firm where he worked. Piotrowski told her and the other articling students that he planned to move to Ottawa when his articles were over. He intended to complete the Bar Admission Course there and hoped to pursue a career in the Department of Justice.

Piotrowski fulfilled the requirement of the articling experience by the beginning of the summer of 1989. He had left all his unused vacation time until the end. Piotrowski could have remained at the firm throughout the summer, but he opted instead to sell his home in Toronto, pack his bags, and move to Ottawa. The next step in his professional education was the completion of the Bar Admission Course, which he was planning to take in Ottawa starting in September. He was hopeful that CSIS would come through with an offer and he would join the recruit training program after graduation. However, if that did not work out, his contingency plan was to seek employment in the federal civil service. Most lawyers who wish to join the federal bureaucracy tend to apply to the Department of Justice. However, Piotrowski was not interested in practicing law and working as a lawyer. After his primary interest in national security, his secondary field of interest was public policy. Moving to Ottawa at that time seemed like a logical thing to do. He visited the City one weekend in the late winter and with the help of a real estate agent visited several condominium apartments in the suburbs of Ottawa that were on the market. On Saturday night he put in an offer on one condo that he liked. By Sunday afternoon he had a contract with a closing date that would permit him to move in when his articles in Toronto were finished. The property he bought was smaller and cost less than what he sold his Toronto home for. Piotrowski had a small mortgage on the new condo and some surplus cash. He planned to use the cash reserves to carry him through the Bar Admission Course.

Just before leaving Toronto Piotrowski thought he should inform the people he had dealt with at CSIS about his impending change of address as Onions suggested. One of the persons he called was Goodale. At the end of the conversation Piotrowski thanked her again for the interview as a polite way of ending the call. Making that call turned out to be a mistake. Trying to be helpful was counterproductive. Instead of just writing a note about Piotrowski's new address for her file she sent the recruiting office a message about Piotrowski's "unusual" communication.

Shortly after Piotrowski arrived in Ottawa he contacted Bob Kaplan at his office on Parliament Hill. Kaplan invited Piotrowski to his office in the Centre Block, just to the right of the main entrance. It was an amazing location, just down the hall from the House of Commons. Kaplan immediately proposed an arrangement whereby former Liberal Party President Senator Robert Stanbury would hire Piotrowski using the budget that all Senators have for the hiring of assistants (but which many Senators did not use) and Piotrowski would mostly work for Kaplan on a variety of projects. What a wonderful opportunity to get some exposure to the inner workings of an MP's office on Parliament Hill! Piotrowski was grateful and thrilled to have this opportunity. Among other things, Kaplan asked Piotrowski to research and draft his submission to the new Commission of Inquiry into Electoral Law Reform. Piotrowski attended and observed many of the Commission's hearings and heard the testimony of many interesting witnesses. Observing the operations of the Commission and its hearings was a great education. He particularly enjoyed analyzing the way some of the more articulate and persuasive witnesses would convey their messages to the Commission members and deal with thorny questions.

At the same time Piotrowski was able to access the Library of Parliament and all its resources. Piotrowski discovered that the library maintained a historic media clipping service and corresponding files on an unlimited number of topics. Piotrowski thought he had found a gold mine when he came across the bulging files on national security, the RCMP Security Service and CSIS. One of the things that he loved doing that summer was rummaging through the library's files and making photocopies of articles that were of interest. Those media clipping files proved to be a valuable resource and source of information.

Another person who Piotrowski contacted upon arriving in Ottawa was Suzanne Guibault. She was happy to reconnect with Piotrowski in Ottawa and invited him over for a coffee. She had moved back in with her partner in a rented townhouse in the West end of Ottawa and was looking for work while temporarily working part-time in a retail store in a large shopping centre. Piotrowski met Guibault and her partner at their home. He detected that there was some tension between them. Her partner appeared to be an average guy who was past his prime and not particularly communicative. Piotrowski was happy to be in touch with Guibault. She was a kind and pleasant lady and he was grateful to her for helping him to prepare for his French language tests. There was also another consideration on Piotrowski's mind. He was unsure of the nature of Guibault's relationship with CSIS. He thought it might be conceivable that she might have been asked by CSIS to observe him and report on him. Although unlikely, it was possible. Accordingly, he felt it was in his interests to be on good terms with her.

About a month after Piotrowski moved to Ottawa Guibault called him. She was sobbing on the phone and in a desperate situation. Her relationship with her partner had hit rock bottom and was irretrievably beyond salvation. He had cheated on her and was no longer interested in her. She had to move out. Yet, she had no place to go. She asked Piotrowski if he would let her stay with him on a temporary basis. Piotrowski was stunned. Guibault was a kind and open lady. Piotrowski and she were on pleasant terms and he sometimes felt like they had known each other for a long time. However, he had only met her a few months earlier and had just moved to Ottawa. He could not believe that she was from Ottawa and did not know anyone else that she could count on. She listed a number of people whom she thought were close to her but could not ask them for help in the circumstances.

Then Piotrowski wondered. Was this CSIS' idea? Could it possibly be that she had been tasked with getting to know Piotrowski up close and rummaging through his files when he was out? Piotrowski thought the idea preposterous. Yet, he could not rule it out. CSIS should have known that it was unnecessary as Piotrowski would have been happy to let them rummage through his possessions at any time. He had nothing to hide from them and thought they might appreciate his library more than anyone else he knew. Piotrowski also wondered if he refused her request that she might inform CSIS and they might conclude that he had something to hide. Piotrowski also thought about what his father's advice might be in such circumstances. His father would probably say "be benevolent". So Piotrowski told her she was welcome. One of the smaller rooms at his condo already had a bed in it.

Guibault moved in the next day. They both tried to make the best of the situation. The more Guibault revealed about her background and her situation, the more Piotrowski realized that she was starting over her adult life from scratch. She had been a traditional housewife and mother who was repressed and behaved for the pleasure of others, not herself. In a mid-life crisis she walked away from it all and was committed to being true to herself and her feelings. She sought independence and happiness for the remainder of her life. Unfortunately, she was struggling and had nothing to her name but a few pieces of furniture, several bags of clothes and her integrity. Piotrowski wanted to be helpful but did not want to become Guibault's crutch.

One weekend a niece of Guibault's was getting married in a small town in Quebec. Guibault asked Piotrowski if he would like to go with her to the wedding at the church and the evening dinner celebration. It would require them to stay in a hotel overnight as the town was a significant distance away. The affair was enjoyable. However, that evening the two settled in separate twin beds in a small country hotel. As they settled to go to sleep, Guibault started crying. Piotrowski tried to say a few comforting words, but he was becoming uncomfortable. Then Guibault reached over from her bed to hold his hand. At that moment Piotrowski decided that this arrangement had to stop. She needed more attention than he was able and willing to give. She was Piotrowski's mother's age and reminded him of her. Any romantic aspirations were out of the question. Whatever CSIS' idea was, they blew it. After their return to Ottawa Piotrowski asked Guibault to find herself another place to stay. Within a week she moved to a friend's home at the other end of town. Piotrowski was relieved.

Shortly after starting to work on Parliament Hill Piotrowski contacted and visited the offices of the Communications Branch of CSIS. The Communications offices of Government departments sometimes have interesting publications about their respective ministries. The CSIS Communications office was the public face of CSIS. It also had the job of scanning the media to keep on top of what was being said in public about CSIS. Piotrowski visited the office which was on the ground floor next to the lobby entrance of the former Veterans' Affairs building on Wellington Street across from the Supreme Court of Canada and just a few blocks from Parliament Hill. The first time Piotrowski visited their office he brought with him a copy of his article in the ISI journal which he thought they might enjoy if they had not seen it already. During that first visit Piotrowski was also hoping to find out if they had any documents (e.g., copies of the latest speeches of the Director, reports, etc.) that he could obtain. In the process, Piotrowski met a CSIS officer named Desmond Greywood and his boss Barry Lemmings, who appeared to be the manager of the Communications office. Besides the CSIS Director who occasionally was the subject of media stories, it was Lemmings who frequently provided CSIS comments on media stories (mostly consisting of the short "neither confirm nor deny" or "no comment" variety). Both officers were courteous and gave Piotrowski positive feedback about his article that they were familiar with. Piotrowski picked up a few copies of some official speeches transcripts and brochures that he had not seen before. Greywood told Piotrowski that he was welcome to come by and pick up other documents as they become available.

That summer Piotrowski developed a routine of spending one or two lunch hours a week visiting the multitude of new and used books stores within walking distance of Parliament Hill either in the market area or on the Sparks Street Mall. He would often find remaindered books on sale at the new book stores or some out-of-print ones at the used book stores. He kept building his library with national security and history related books.

Sometimes he would have a couple of books that he had just bought and pop into the CSIS Communications office to see Greywood and ask if there were any new speeches or documents that were available. Sometimes he would have a short friendly chat with Greywood of the "How ya doin'? What's new?" variety. If Piotrowski had just picked up a special book he might show it to Greywood or talk about the last one he had read. Piotrowski was always on the lookout for some tips regarding the publicly available literature about CSIS and espionage generally and was interested in finding out which books CSIS considered to be authoritative. Unfortunately, neither Greywood nor Lemmings were particularly willing to make any pronouncements on the topic and Piotrowski did not ask any probing questions and risk any discomfort. Later Piotrowski would discover that reading books was not something they did much of. A little later a new book came out about CSIS and Piotrowski asked Lemmings what he thought of it. Lemmings replied that he had not read the book and appeared to be satisfied with just reading a book review about it.

CHAPTER 7:
THE PANEL INTERVIEW

Before moving to Ottawa Piotrowski was informed that the person in the CSIS Human Resources Department who was in charge of recruiting was Richard Latrappe. Shortly after his arrival in Ottawa Piotrowski was contacted by Latrappe's office and invited to a panel interview. From what Piotrowski understood about the recruiting process, this was the final interview. Piotrowski had previously found a copy of a newspaper article about the CSIS recruitment process in which the CSIS Communications Director Lemmings was quoted as suggesting that the questions posed at this panel interview were "tough". The previous year Piotrowski met a CSIS librarian at a CASIS conference and kept in touch with him. One day they met over lunch in the Parliamentary Hill cafeteria and discussed recently-published literature about espionage. Piotrowski asked him about the newspaper article and the recruiting process without divulging that he was an applicant. The CSIS librarian told him "anyone who made it to that stage was as good as accepted." Piotrowski liked the sound of that. He was looking forward to the panel interview and the "tough" questions that the panel would throw at him.

A week later he showed up at the designated CSIS location and was ushered into a board meeting room. On one side of the large rectangular table were the three panel members while Piotrowski sat opposite. The three panel members were three men, Richard Latrappe, Jean Goblet, and Serge Fortin. Piotrowski was happy to finally meet Latrappe in person after having previously spoken with him on the phone several times. Latrappe was in his early forties. The other two were older veterans who looked like experienced RCMP and CSIS officers who were about a week away from retirement. All three were French.

Piotrowski brought copies of his recently published article in the International Security Institute's journal to the panel interview. Piotrowski had previously sent one to the Latrappe. He gave a copy to the two older gentlemen and another one to Latrappe so it would not appear that he was leaving him out. The two older officers seemed to enthusiastically receive it and showed an interest in it as they flipped through the pages. That was a refreshing contrast to the rebuff that Gendron had previously given Piotrowski at their previous meeting.

Although Piotrowski expected to be asked some challenging questions, he found the questions rather general and easy to deal with. Why did he want to join CSIS? Piotrowski had already answered that question several times. What did he think the Service's role was? He referred to the Act. What did he think were the greatest threats to Canadian national security? He referred to the definition of the threats in the Act and discussed them at length with examples. One of the things he mentioned was the need for the economy to generate wealth and for the political system to ensure an appropriate amount of fair distribution. He suggested that if the economy were ever to experience another profound downturn, as during the Great Depression of the 1930s, we could expect extremists who did not believe in liberal democracy to become increasingly appealing to a greater portion of the population because they may be perceived as offering solutions which the incumbent institutions did not. Piotrowski referred to the heyday of the communists and Adrien Arcand's fascists in the thirties. Whether these were domestic subversive movements or foreign-influenced, they would have greater appeal and success during a prolonged period of economic crisis. The panel members nodded and took notes.

Then they asked Piotrowski about how he would deal with certain situations that they described. Piotrowski tried to flag all the relevant legal, ethical and security issues in each case scenario to show them that he was aware of what the issues were and what the potential ramifications could be before suggesting what his proposed approach to each scenario would be. The panel members kept on taking notes and occasionally Goblet and Fortin would smile.

Piotrowski left the panel confident that he had done well, but wondering "*Was that it? Are Canadian intelligence officers really recruited on the basis of such superficial interviews?*" Piotrowski had this nagging thought that there was something remarkably shallow about what he had just been through. Apart from the strange interview with the oddball "psychologist" Gendron, none of the interviews or tests were challenging in any way and the whole process struck Piotrowski as vapid. He wondered how much did CSIS really learn about the candidates during the recruiting process. He knew that background security checks were being made. Obviously, the information that the field investigators were collecting would supplement what CSIS interviewers learned directly from him. But if the field investigators were doing as superficial a job as the interviewers that he encountered were doing, he started having doubts about the quality and reliability of what they had in their files and the basis upon which they made their decisions. Piotrowski was surprised that at no time did a CSIS officer show up at his door to ask to see where and how he lived. He would have been happy to let them in. Evidently, they did not care and were not interested. He would later find out how his misgivings were justified.

Piotrowski was informed that nothing further was required of him. He crossed his fingers and hoped that an offer of employment would be forthcoming.

CHAPTER 8:
WAITING

At the end of the summer of 1989, Piotrowski ceased working for Senator Stanbury and Bob Kaplan and began the Bar Admission Course which was given by the Law Society of Upper Canada at their facilities close to downtown. The Bar Admission Course involved consecutive intense three-week courses in different subjects followed by exams. Around that time the federal Government appointed a committee of MPs, known as the Thacker Committee (named after its chairman Blaine Thacker) to conduct the review of the *CSIS Act* as required by the five-year review clause. Piotrowski reflected on the letter he previously received from CSIS Deputy Director Harry Brandes encouraging him to make a submission to the Committee. After observing the proceedings of the Royal Commission on Electoral Law Reform, preparing a submission to this Parliamentary *CSIS Act* Review Committee struck Piotrowski as a once-in-a-lifetime opportunity which would be an exciting endeavour. Anyone who makes a submission may also have an opportunity to appear as a witness before the Committee. Given the controversial nature of CSIS and its business, as well as the variety of political stripes on the Committee, there could be some interesting sparks at such hearings as different perspectives on critical issues may clash.

However, Piotrowski's priority was to seek employment with CSIS first and foremost. Accordingly, as Onions told Piotrowski that he could write and publish or say anything he wanted but that he should not reveal that he was a CSIS applicant, Piotrowski was willing to pursue the project. Nonetheless, to be on the safe side, Piotrowski contacted Latrappe and informed him of his desire to make a submission to the Thacker Committee. Piotrowski told him that if there was any conflict or risk of jeopardizing his candidacy he would gladly and without any hesitation cease and desist from the activity and forget about it. Latrappe provided no feedback either way. He gave Piotrowski the impression that he did not care. At no point was Piotrowski warned or discouraged from engaging in the endeavour.

Accordingly, Piotrowski decided to prepare a submission to the Committee. The basic theme of the submission would be the same as in the ISI journal article, namely, the balance between national security and civil liberties was more or less appropriately set and did not require any major adjustments. To make the case that CSIS should not have its powers diminished, Piotrowski tried to document examples of the threats to our national security as much as possible. Those library media clipping files were an invaluable source of such examples as Piotrowski came across a number of examples that he was not previously aware of and he included many examples in the appendices.

Piotrowski told both Greywood and Lemmings that he was preparing a submission to the Thacker Committee and wondered if they would like to see a draft and possibly comment on it before it was finalized. He also told them that he was an applicant to CSIS. He hoped that by having the CSIS Communications Branch review a draft of the manuscript he would be minimizing and avoiding the risk of including something that may be false or problematic in any way. After discussing it amongst themselves, Greywood told Piotrowski that they would be happy to review and comment on Piotrowski's draft submission to the Review Committee, but strictly on an "informal basis". Once Piotrowski had a sufficiently developed draft he provided Greywood with a copy. Greywood consulted with his co-workers. A week later Greywood provided Piotrowski with some feedback. The comments consisted of a number of minor suggestions for changes. Nothing major. All the comments were editorial in nature and mostly concerned sentence structure and grammar. The message that Piotrowski understood was that the content was "good to go".

Piotrowski would later read in his CSIS file that this project was an example of behaviour that demonstrated that Piotrowski could not be trusted. The file contained no mention of his providing notice to Latrappe and effectively asking him for permission. Similarly, it contained no mention of the fact that he gave an advance copy to the CSIS Communication Branch and that it effectively vetted and endorsed the submission.

Once Piotrowski had finalized the submission, he sent it to the Committee. In Piotrowski's cover letter he indicated that he would be pleased to appear as a witness before the Committee to elaborate on the submission should the Committee members provide him with that opportunity. Piotrowski also sent the submission to Latrappe for inclusion in his application file and to the CSIS Communications Branch for their records. He was quite proud of the document as it contained a comprehensive overview of documented threats to Canadian National Security and what he thought was a reasonable and balanced discussion of the *CSIS Act* and whether or not it needed to be amended.

A few weeks later Piotrowski received a phone call from a CBC radio producer for the daily national *Morningside* show with host Peter Gzowski. The CBC was planning to put together a panel of three "experts" on national security to discuss the review of the *CSIS Act* on one episode in the near future. The CBC producer had come across Piotrowski's ISI journal article and invited Piotrowski to be a panelist along with Peter Russell and Alan Borovoy. Both names were familiar to anyone who had studied the history of the debates around Canadian intelligence and security. Peter Russell was a professor at the University of Toronto and Alan Borovoy was the general counsel to the Canadian Civil Liberties Association. Piotrowski was thrilled to have an opportunity to be on the program. He was being given a chance to debate two of the most powerful authorities and occasional critics of CSIS and the *CSIS Act* on national radio. The weekday program aired between 9:00 a.m. and 12 noon and had an audience of a few hundred thousand. The show would be live (not pre-recorded).

Again, Piotrowski contacted Latrappe to inform him that he was given this opportunity to discuss the reform of the *CSIS Act* on the CBC. Again, Piotrowski told Latrappe that if he were to tell him that such participation in the radio program would be a risk or jeopardize his application, he would cancel his appearance. Again, Latrappe provided no feedback either way. Piotrowski also informed Greywood in the Communications Branch and gave him a head's up in case he and his colleagues might wish to tune in.

A few days later, Piotrowski attended the CBC Radio studios which were located on the top floors of the Chateau Laurier in Ottawa. Piotrowski was taken to a studio where he was sitting in front of a microphone and had a set of headphones. Piotrowski was alone, as the host and the two other guests were in the Toronto studio. This put Piotrowski at a disadvantage as he could not see their body language or "off–air" communication and signals. Piotrowski was nervous as he had never done something like this before. It was exciting. Such panels are set up to usually reflect differences of opinion. As the other panelists clearly wanted to "err" on the side of caution and further restrict CSIS powers, the producers had clearly hoped to use Piotrowski to provide the clash of ideas. Piotrowski happily adopted the position of erring on the side of caution and not further restricting CSIS powers. The segment lasted about twenty minutes. When it was over Piotrowski thought he had done well and was proud of himself. After years of research and study of the subject matter it was personally satisfying for Piotrowski to be able to engage in skirmishes in defence of CSIS with two leading authorities on live national radio.

Shortly after the radio appearance, Piotrowski contacted Greywood who politely congratulated him. Greywood told Piotrowski that they listened to it and thought he did well. Greywood then told Piotrowski that they had transcripts of the program. Piotrowski asked him if he could have a copy. He was thinking that not only would he like a copy for his records, but he wanted to bring it to the attention of Latrappe and ensure that a copy got into his application file. Surely the recruiting personnel would be interested in how a candidate was able to discuss the national security and the *CSIS Act* on live national radio with two of the service's authoritative critics.

When Piotrowski went to the Communications office to get a copy of the transcript Lemmings told him that it was good that he was on the program because such programs historically always trotted out the same old critics with the same old messages. He suggested that it was good to have some new blood in the public discourse with fresh perspectives and he seemed to thank Piotrowski without actually saying so. When Greywood gave Piotrowski a copy of the transcripts he added a cover note in which he handwrote "Thanks for your efforts to balance the public record." Lemmings and Greywood seemed to appreciate what he had done which benefited the Service. Piotrowski thought that was a positive sign. Only later would he find out what CSIS really thought of it all. It would not be good.

Piotrowski then contacted Latrappe and told him that he had the transcript of his appearance on the CBC radio program and would like to deliver a copy to add to his application file. Latrappe gave Piotrowski the address of their offices (this was before their new modern office building was built in the East end of Ottawa) and told Piotrowski that he could show up at the front desk to make the delivery. The next day Piotrowski went to the office building and informed the Commissionaire at the front desk that he had something for the personnel department. He took Piotrowski's name, made a phone call, and asked him to wait in the lobby area. A few moments later a CSIS employee emerged into the lobby area from behind a secured and closed door.

The man was an average size gentleman around forty years old. He had a scruffy beard and was wearing a brown suit that looked like the standard uniform in the Government civil service. From the moment that he emerged from behind the closed door he looked at me in a penetrating and strange manner. He stared at me with wide-open eyes as if I was an unusual lifeform from another planet. He asked me if I was Chris Piotrowski. I said I was. The man then introduced himself as Victor Goulet and shook my hand. I told Goulet that I was recently on a CBC radio program discussing CSIS and that I had a copy of the transcripts which I wanted to ask that he kindly add to my application file. Goulet took the document from me without hesitation and continued to look at me in an odd way which started to make me feel uncomfortable. Then Goulet said, "I've read your recent paper on CSIS." I smiled and did not quite know what to say so I just thanked him. "It's very good" he added. I thought was a good sign. But then Goulet added something with ominous undertones which I did not fully appreciate at the time. Goulet said, "You know more about CSIS than the people who work here." I thought it was a compliment at the time. I should have recognized it as the dangerous warning sign that it was. All of my knowledge about CSIS and Canadian national security came from reading open-source information and my meetings and encounters with people either in the business or academics. If I knew more about CSIS than people who work there, what did that say about the people that work there? Would people who have been comfortable in a job and organization for years want to bring on board some new recruit who knows more about the organization and its mandate than they do?

The *Privacy Act* file that CSIS subsequently provided Piotrowski did not contain any record of his having contacted Latrappe to inform him of the invitation he received to appear on the program, a copy of the transcript of the program, or any commentary on it. Similarly, there was no commentary reflecting Goulet's comments about Piotrowski's publication that he had read or his comment about Piotrowski's knowledge of CSIS. Instead, there was repeated commentary stating that Piotrowski's "high profile" activities were proof that he could not be trusted and would be unlikely to abide by the non-disclosure of employment rule.

During that summer of 1989 something remarkable happened in Poland. The Communist Government held elections in the country and actually permitted the Solidarity union to run as an opposition party. Solidarity won. This was a first in a Soviet-dominated Communist country. It was effectively the first event in that tumultuous period which was punctuated by the collapse of the Berlin Wall and the Iron Curtain, and terminated with the disintegration of the Soviet empire and the U.S.S.R. Since leaving Poland in 1960 Piotrowski's father has been a participant in Polish ethnic affairs and he was a senior official of the Polish Canadian Congress. His father never wanted to visit Poland while it was a Communist state. However, during the first free elections in that summer of 1989, he returned on a visit to Poland for the first time since leaving Poland decades earlier. He had already scheduled a sabbatical for the following year. Instead, he changed his plans and returned to Poland for several months in 1990 where he tried to contribute to the political reforms there. Many of his former university colleagues were now politicians with the Solidarity movement and he participated in many meetings and discussions about the future of Poland.

Piotrowski was very concerned about how CSIS would view his father's ethnic community political activities and trips to Poland. So he asked his father to meet with somebody at CSIS' regional office in Montreal before and after his trips to explain that he was the father of an applicant and to tell them what he was doing so that there would not be any unnecessary suspicion around his application. Piotrowski's father subsequently informed him that he met a total of four times with a CSIS officer in Montreal by the name of "Daniel" and that the meetings were informative and went well. Daniel was interested in hearing from Piotrowski's father about the developments in Poland and his involvement.

When Piotrowski's father confirmed to him that he met with a CSIS officer in Montreal, Piotrowski contacted Latrappe and informed him that his father had met with somebody from CSIS in Montreal regarding his involvement in Polish politics and ethnic community involvement. Latrappe expressed surprise at learning that Piotrowski's father was active in the Polish community. Piotrowski was surprised that Latrappe was surprised. This further added to Piotrowski's impression that the investigation into his background was done in a cursory manner. Despite all his candour and the information that he provided CSIS, they knew little about him. One got the impression that the left hand did not know what the right hand was doing and that getting the full and complete story was not the objective. When Piotrowski subsequently received his CSIS application file there was no mention of his father's meetings with CSIS in Montreal.

Piotrowski diligently worked on his Bar Admission Course studies and passed all the exams. The last exam was on February 28, 1990. The formal Call to the Bar ceremony took place at the National Arts Centre in March. Piotrowski was glad when it was over. His hope was that the offer from CSIS would come during that period and that he would start working at CSIS in 1990. However, from CSIS there was only silence and he began to worry. He remembered the CSIS librarian who had told him that anyone invited to a panel interview he was as good as in. What was taking so long?

In early 1990, a full year after his initial CSIS interview with Onions, Piotrowski called and spoke with Latrappe about the status of his application. Latrappe told Piotrowski that the security clearance was being worked on and that he had monthly meetings with the responsible people. He told Piotrowski that if Piotrowski wanted to get updated on the situation he should call him monthly. In a subsequent conversation Latrappe told Piotrowski he could call him semi-monthly for updates. He encouraged Piotrowski to do this. Unfortunately, Latrappe always responded the same way to Piotrowski's inquiries and repeatedly told him that the process was "ongoing" and he should call back again in two weeks.

Based on information in SIRC reports about the average length of time CSIS took to complete security clearances, Piotrowski knew that his was already beyond the average. Having been told by Latrappe that the only thing holding up the offer was a security clearance, he was of course anxious about the delay, but confident that the offer would come as there was no reason to deny him a security clearance.

Once Piotrowski finished with school he was in a strange holding pattern as he waited for CSIS to complete the security clearance investigation and for the offer of employment to come through. Piotrowski realized that there was no guarantee that CSIS would offer him a job. He understood that he might be rejected and need to pursue a career elsewhere. However, he did not see any point in seeking employment elsewhere as he anticipated that the CSIS offer would be coming soon. If he did look for other work he had no doubt that he would quit whatever it was as soon as he got the CSIS offer. However, as the weeks dragged on, Piotrowski realized that some temporary work would be useful. Piotrowski had kept in touch with Bob Kaplan and he again kindly offered Piotrowski a contract to join his office staff as a research assistant during the spring and summer. Piotrowski was more than happy to contribute to various projects that Kaplan was working on. Piotrowski particularly enjoyed attending meetings with Kaplan on different matters of public policy as he had a wealth of knowledge garnered throughout his lengthy career and his questions and comments were always educational.

During the period that Piotrowski worked on Parliament Hill in 1990 he resumed his regular walks over the lunch hour to several nearby bookstores. He would also occasionally venture to visit the CSIS Communications office and chat with Greywood and see if there were any new speech transcripts or reports that were available. One day Piotrowski went to the Communication Branch to pick up a new document that was newly released and available. As Piotrowski walked into the office and greeted Greywood the latter had an unusually big smile on his face and looked extremely proud of himself. He then revealed to Piotrowski the source of his pride. Greywood had his own bookstore shopping bag which had a book in it. Greywood had evidently gone to a nearby bookstore on the Sparks Street Mall and bought a book on espionage. Greywood behaved as though this was a new experience for him and although he did not say it, Piotrowski got the impression that this unprecedented behaviour was a result of Piotrowski's influence. Piotrowski smiled back and exchanged some pleasantries with Greywood and wished him much enjoyment while reading the book.

Throughout the encounter and afterward Piotrowski thought about what had just happened which struck him as pathetic. An intelligence officer was beaming like a kid with a new toy because he had bought a book. And not just any book, but one about espionage. Evidently, this was not a common occurrence or normal practice. The incident made Piotrowski feel uncomfortable as it suggested that exhausting open-source information and reading background history, which was fundamental to understanding any serious international conflict and the current state of affairs, was not something that came naturally, at least not for some RCMP veterans and officers at CSIS. No wonder Goulet had previously looked at Piotrowski like a Martian and claimed Piotrowski knew more about CSIS than people who work there! Piotrowski later learned that Greywood had joined the RCMP after graduating from high school. Greywood would go on to rise within the CSIS hierarchy to a very senior position. Years later Greywood would retire from CSIS and become a consultant. Occasionally Greywood would be seen on television commenting on national security issues. Whenever Piotrowski recognized Greywood on television he was reminded of Greywood's smile and pride over the purchase of an espionage book.

One day during the Spring of 1990 Piotrowski was contacted by a CSIS agent named Stewart Fowler. He called to invite Piotrowski to a hotel room to discuss a matter. Piotrowski assumed that this had to do with his application and specifically with his security clearance. Fowler did not give any details on the phone about what the issues were to be discussed. Piotrowski thought this was a good development and he invited Fowler to his home instead. Fowler was not initially receptive to the idea but when Piotrowski suggested to him that since they are doing a security clearance investigation on him, he would be very happy to have Fowler come to his home and CSIS could save itself the cost of renting a hotel room. Fowler eventually reluctantly agreed.

Piotrowski looked forward to the meeting and clearing up whatever concern that CSIS may have had about his background. At the agreed-upon day and time Fowler showed up at Piotrowski's home. Fowler was a middle-aged veteran from the RCMP days and struck Piotrowski as a little rough around the edges. He was somewhat frosty and stiff. Piotrowski offered him something to drink and put some cookies on a plate. Fowlers declined everything, including a glass of water. He then proceeded to ask Piotrowski about his time at McGill University. He got to the heart of the matter and asked Piotrowski whether he was aware of any foreign influenced activities on campus. Piotrowski replied that he was aware of a lot of left-wing student activism, but not aware of any specific instances where he could identify a student or a student organization or club specifically being directed by foreign agents. There were many left-wing individuals and organizations on campus that constantly put up posters and inserted stories in the student papers that would contain anti-American, anti-NATO and anti-capitalist type of messages, while simultaneously praising or falsely misrepresenting Soviet policy, etc. This was common. However, Piotrowski could not say that there was any direct or even indirect Soviet manipulation involved and he certainly had no evidence or proof of foreign influenced activities on campus. Piotrowski described how he wrote an opinion piece in the student paper questioning the peaceniks' incessant promotion of unilateral disarmament and how it resulted in a lengthy back and forth debate in the paper with an anti-American Soviet sympathizer. Piotrowski told Fowler that there are so many people similar to what Lenin referred to as "useful idiots" that surreptitious Soviet influence is often unnecessary to promote Soviet interests (or at least what the Soviets perceived to be in their interests).

Fowler seemed unsatisfied with Piotrowski's answer and continued to repeat his question about whether Piotrowski was aware of any foreign meddling. Again, Piotrowski repeated that he knew of none. Piotrowski then asked about the status of my security clearance and Fowler's face went blank. Piotrowski then realized that

Fowler's calling him had nothing to do with his application to CSIS but was part of some sort of other separate investigation and Fowler was on a fishing trip. When Piotrowski told Fowler that he was hoping to do the kind of work Fowler was doing someday and that he'd been through the interviews, was waiting for the security clearance, could not think about what was causing the delay, and thought that Fowler's contacting him had to do with his application, Fowler became rather hostile and blurted out *"CSIS is not a meal ticket!"* in a rather dismissive tone. Piotrowski was stunned. Was Fowler implying that Piotrowski was looking to CSIS for welfare and was unworthy of consideration as a candidate? Piotrowski tried to politely point out that he did not need any meal tickets and his interest in national security had nothing to do with welfare. Fowler was clearly unhappy that he was no further ahead in his investigation of whatever it was he was investigating and had come all the way from the Montreal office for nothing and left.

Piotrowski was perplexed by the experience. Piotrowski did not understand how it was possible that he sincerely wanted to help Fowler (and CSIS) in his quest and instead of recognizing an ally, Fowler insulted him by suggesting that he was just looking for a "meal ticket". Piotrowski tried to be as honest and truthful as he could be. He was unaware of any specific foreign influenced activity on campus at the time that he was there. Period. Just because Fowler kept repeating his question and pressuring Piotrowski to come up with something, he wasn't going to make something up or list the names of well-known leftist student activists and imply something nefarious about which he had no proof. The CSIS file that Piotrowski obtained did not contain a word about Fowler's visit and investigation. But it did contain repeated comments that Piotrowski was an extremist that could not be expected to be objective and trustworthy. Fowler's offensive comment was only the first of many derogatory comments that Piotrowski would subsequently discover in his application file.

In April Piotrowski received an invitation to appear before the Thacker Committee in May as a witness. Piotrowski contacted the

Committee Clerk and was informed that if Piotrowski accepted the invitation, he would be part of a panel of three witnesses. The other two were academics from two separate universities. Each of the three witnesses would be given a maximum of ten minutes to make an opening statement. This would be followed by questions from the committee members. This was an exciting opportunity to participate in the democratic and political process. Again, Piotrowski informed Latrappe that he had received this invitation and told him that if this would in any way jeopardize his application he would gladly cancel his participation. Latrappe said nothing. Piotrowski also informed Greywood in the Communications Branch to give them advance notice as a courtesy, although they were monitoring the Committee's work and would eventually find out if they did not already know.

My experience as a witness before the committee was very satisfying. The other two witnesses were older academics who I knew of and whose works I was familiar with. Both of them addressed CSIS wrongdoings and used SIRC reports and media stories to suggest that CSIS should have less power and be subjected to more red tape. I was the third to speak and in my opening statement I covered the main highlights of my submission and made the case that no more red tape was necessary. The Committee Chair then moderated the question period. Each MP on the Committee was allocated the same time period for asking questions of the witnesses. Each of the Committee members already had a copy of my written submission. The NDP Justice critic on the committee engaged me in a debate on several points in my submission and we had a lively exchange that by most accounts was a draw. I was very happy to have had this experience. To be honest, it was exciting and I was proud of my having stood up for what I believed and that I was able to explain it and defend it.

Eventually the Committee released the transcripts of the session and Piotrowski obtained a few copies. He made sure to deliver one to Latrappe for insertion in his application file. Latrappe provided no feedback or comment and Piotrowski would later discover that there was no mention or analysis of his appearance before the Committee in his CSIS application file, apart from the repeated comments that his writing and speaking was demonstrable evidence that Piotrowski would be unable to keep a secret.

Piotrowski also sent one copy of the transcript of his appearance to the first Director of CSIS, Ted Finn, who was now the Director of Emergency Preparedness Canada. His offices were in downtown Ottawa just a few blocks away from Parliament Hill. Finn kindly replied and offered Piotrowski some encouraging and positive feedback. In a letter to Piotrowski dated June 26, 1990, Finn wrote "I want to thank you for sending me a copy of the proceedings of the 'Special Committee' before which you appeared [...] I was quite frankly impressed by the breadth of your statement and the manner in which you fielded the questions put to you. Keep up the good work."

Piotrowski followed up and was fortunate enough to have a meeting with Finn in his office. When he met Finn he reminded him of their first brief encounter at the law school conference when Finn delivered a keynote address. Finn suggested to Piotrowski that he should seriously consider a career in academia. He gave Piotrowski the impression that he thought that the academic community was frequently misguided and having some new academics with Piotrowski's perspectives might be helpful. Piotrowski appreciated Finn's suggestion. Piotrowski was happy to have had the opportunity to meet and discuss the status of the *CSIS Act* with the former CSIS Director. Piotrowski's CSIS file would not contain any reference to the meeting or any reference of the former Director's positive review of Piotrowski's appearance before the Committee. Instead, Piotrowski's file would describe him as "vain", "narcissistic" and suggest that he "was in constant need of admiration and attention".

Piotrowski also sent a copy of his submission and testimony transcripts to W.H. Kelly, the former Deputy Commissioner of the RCMP. Piotrowski had previously met Kelly and asked him to autograph several of Kelly's books about the history of the RCMP. Piotrowski later received a letter from Kelly dated July 7, 1990, in which he wrote: "I have read with great interest your [...written submission and testimony transcript...] I must say that I was impressed with the pertinence of your conclusions in both instances, particularly as all your sources were public. I am sure that CSIS with its sources, both public and secret, and ample research facilities, could not have provided the committee with a more objective view of the present situation. It follows from this that I would be more than surprised if CSIS, in any way, would disagree with your views and your conclusions. I must congratulate you on your efforts in this regard, and hope that you will continue to put your knowledge of these matters before the Canadian public."

Although Kelly thought the content of Piotrowski's submission and testimony was objective, CSIS investigators and analysts would express doubt as to Piotrowski's ability to be objective if he were to work for the Service or anywhere else.

By July 1990 Piotrowski was becoming increasingly worried that there was some sort of a problem with his security clearance. He was sure that whatever CSIS was concerned about the matter could be cleared up if they would contact him and ask about it. Piotrowski read in the SIRC annual report that the average length of time to get a "Top Secret" clearance was eight months and so far his had taken twice that long with no news about how long it would drag on for. Piotrowski decided to call Goodale in Toronto to inquire about the status of his security clearance. That was a big mistake. Goodale told him that she had no idea. Piotrowski would later discover that she wrote a memo about his call that was included in the application file. The memo implied that Piotrowski was impatient. Piotrowski then called Onions who expressed surprise and said "I thought you were already in".

At this time Piotrowski figured he had nothing to lose by contacting one of the security clearance investigators who had previously met with one of Piotrowski's references in Ottawa. On this list of references Piotrowski included an old family friend who knew Piotrowski since he was a child. The CSIS investigator, Stewart Duncan, visited Piotrowski's friend about six months earlier and left his card with the reference. The friend called Piotrowski after the interview and told him about the question she was asked about him including whether Piotrowski drank, took drugs, and what he thought of democracy. The friend also said she informed the investigator that Piotrowski had moved to Ottawa and lived in a nearby neighbourhood, which surprised the investigator. Evidently, Piotrowski's informing CSIS of his move from Toronto to Ottawa was not something that was shared with the Ottawa investigator. She also showed him a copy of Piotrowski's recent article about the reform of CSIS which Piotrowski had previously given her. The friend subsequently gave Duncan's card to Piotrowski.

Piotrowski decided to call Duncan to see if there was anything he could learn about the delay. Duncan was very friendly and said he enjoyed reading Piotrowski's article which he found out about from Piotrowski's friend and subsequently got his own copy. Unfortunately, he could not tell Piotrowski anything about the status of the application. However, he encouraged Piotrowski to keep in touch. Piotrowski was encouraged by Duncan's kindness. Later, Duncan would actually invite Piotrowski to his home for dinner with him and his wife one evening and tell him about his career. Duncan had plenty of interesting stories about his encounters with Pierre Trudeau and other Parliamentarians. Duncan gave Piotrowski a drive home afterward in a Buick from the early 1970s that was in mint condition with so many features from the seat to the dashboard that reminded Piotrowski of his youth. Duncan obviously took good care of his car but claimed that he never had to do anything exceptional for maintenance apart from occasionally having to replace a spark plug.

It had now been months since Piotrowski had finished school and the continued waiting was starting to have a depressing effect on his spirits. However, he would not have to wait much longer.

CHAPTER 9:
REJECTION AT LAST

In early September 1990, a full two years since Piotrowski submitted his application to CSIS, 21 months after his first interview and 14 months after the panel interview, he received a letter indicating that he had been rejected. It was a short one-page letter. No reasons were given. It concluded by thanking Piotrowski for his interest. Although Piotrowski was deeply disappointed by the rejection, he was also relieved. As there was such a delay in the processing of his file he increasingly began to suspect the result would be negative. The length of time that CSIS took to come to conclude this matter contributed to the building up of stressful suspense which Piotrowski was glad was over.

Now that Piotrowski knew there was no hope with CSIS, he would have to pursue a career elsewhere. He would begin that quest the next day. He would find another short-term speech-writing contract for Senator Stanbury on Parliament Hill and then in one day in November he would be offered positions in two separate Government Departments. He picked the larger one with greater opportunities. His civil service career in the world of public policy began in early December 1990.

However, the receipt of the rejection letter from CSIS left an unresolved issue. Why? What were the reasons? He could understand being rejected if there were valid reasons against hiring him. What could they be? Could it be that all the other candidates were better? Perhaps. But Piotrowski doubted that. Onions had told him that he was "head and shoulders above the other candidates". Piotrowski wished he could see their test scores and rankings to compare how he did. Could it be that there was something in his background that was a problem? He could not think of anything. If there was a mistake in CSIS' reasoning Piotrowski would at least have liked to know about it and clear it up. Had he made a mistake or series of mistakes? Were they fatal?

Piotrowski immediately decided to make a *Privacy Act* request for his application file. A month later he received notice that CSIS was making use of the extension period that was permitted under the Act. In early November 1990, he received a large thick brown envelope in the mail.

Both days when Piotrowski received the rejection letter and the released parts of the application file were painful ones that had a shocking effect. However, Piotrowski had recently become involved in a relationship with a new girlfriend. They had coincidentally previously scheduled dates on both of those evenings and ended up spending the nights together. Had Piotrowski been alone on those evenings he would have probably had a drink or two. Instead, he woke up each morning with a new sense of *joie de vivre* and fresh courage. A new chapter was starting in Piotrowski's life, but some things had to be wrapped up first.

CHAPTER 10:
THE *PRIVACY ACT* AND THE CSIS FILE

The *Privacy Act* package that contained the released portions of Piotrowski's CSIS application file contained five separate files. The package was about an inch thick. Much of it was edited (redacted) and blacked out.

The cover letter was signed by Hugh Inrun and indicated that the results of the psychological tests were not included in the release. However, the letter indicated that Piotrowski could call a certain telephone number and make an appointment to "consult the results". He immediately did so and scheduled an appointment for two days later.

The *Privacy Act* package contained numerous files and documents, which largely consisted of memos and notes to the file. Some were reports of interviewers who had meetings with Piotrowski. Others were reports of investigators who were gathering information about Piotrowski and his background. Others were memos and reports written by analysts who reviewed the reports and submitted information from the investigators or interviewers and generated some kind of assessment and conclusion or recommendation for management. There were memos providing status reports and information to management. And then there were a number of "transit slip" memo covers and related documents. Many of the documents contained tombstone type of data or factual statements about where Piotrowski was at one time or another.

Presumably, the way the system should work is that the interviewers and investigators should compile all the relevant facts that they had discovered about the person and his or her background that should clearly be distinguished from the interviewers' or investigators' opinions, impressions, and interpretations. Analysts should then be able to review the reports with a view to focusing on the important points and setting aside the irrelevant or minor stuff that had little or no bearing on the overall assessment of the candidate, keeping in mind the context of when and how the information was generated. What may appear to be a minor issue may turn out to be a red flag worthy of more attention, and vice versa. Making that determination is part of the analyst's challenge. Nobody said doing a proper and professional job is easy.

Unfortunately, the opposite consistently occurred throughout the file. An investigator received some negative feedback from a former bartending instructor from a brief period eight years prior when the candidate was still a teenager. Those opinions and out-of-context facts would be emphasized and repeated with increasing emphasis to the point where they assumed the status of undeniable facts. Those "facts", including the perceived character and maturity level of the candidate, were then assumed to have been become even more pronounced throughout the candidate's life to the present day. Had the investigator interviewed Sylvain Gagner or any of his University of Calgary classmates the report from that time in Piotrowski's life would have appeared quite different. Yet, the analyst memos focused on this one source's negative comments as if they were the essence of what the candidate was really like at that time, and all the time since. The fact that Piotrowski's previous bosses, including former Solicitor-General Bob Kaplan, would hire and re-hire Piotrowski in the years since and the most recent past was not mentioned.

Similarly, the analysts would focus on minor trivialities or misinterpretations that they would blow out of proportion while ignoring the big picture or more pertinent facts. For example, during the interview with Goodale she asked Piotrowski to tell her about his parents. While Piotrowski provided her with this information and while speaking about his mother and her education, she suddenly interrupted him and asked about the subject matter of his mother's psychology M.A. thesis from the 1950s at the University of Warsaw. Piotrowski could not remember it. He knew the general subject matter (e.g., psychology and the name of her supervising professor who was a rather famous Polish academic) but he could not remember what the actual thesis topic was. She rarely talked about it. He could get that information by contacting his mother if that were important, but he was not asked to. It is of course conceivable that Goodale asked the question to see if Piotrowski was reciting a false legend and whether she could trip him up somehow. Of course, there was no false legend and what Piotrowski told her could all be verified. Yet, she felt it necessary to document the fact that in 1989 Piotrowski did not know off the top of his head what the specific thesis topic was of his mother's M.A. thesis from 1959 in another country, another language and before Piotrowski was even born. A subsequent analyst used Piotrowski's inability at that moment to confirm the subject of his mother's thesis to conclude that any claim Piotrowski made about being a curious person was "a joke". All other evidence of research, study and pursuit of his interests was irrelevant. Piotrowski blew one question about his mother's thesis topic, and that was conclusive evidence that he was not a curious person and a fraud. Piotrowski knew his father's doctoral thesis topic and told Goodale. However, that was not considered a mitigating factor worthy of mention or comment. What could explain such aberrant reasoning and dismissive attitude from someone who never actually met Piotrowski? Piotrowski wondered if the "analyst" harboured resentment against candidates who had a university education and what was the likelihood that he (or she) and his parents had university degrees.

One of the most disappointing repetitions of errors involved the carelessness with which a number of CSIS officers repeatedly misspelled Piotrowski's first and last names. While Piotrowski was used to "Krzysztof" often appearing in different forms throughout his life, the carelessness and negligence with respect to his last name throughout the file were surprising. In some places it was "Piorkowski", and in others "Piokowsky". In another place it was misspelled as "Piokowzki". Attention to detail and respect for a person's name were not important for a number of people at CSIS. Piotrowski often wondered what would have happened if his last name had an additional syllable or whether his file would have been handled differently if his last name sounded English or French instead of Slavic.

The Onions Report

The file contained a document titled "Personal Suitability Interview" and it was signed by David Onions.

On the first page there is a statement in the assessment section that "*the intensity with which he discusses this field of study borders on being extreme*". The introduction of the word "extreme" was unfortunate. It undoubtedly contributed to subsequent reports and memos alleging Piotrowski to be an "extremist". While it appeared that Onions was trying to say that Piotrowski's interest in the field is intense, the word "extreme" is a red flag that may be easily confused with the content of Piotrowski's discussions. Once such a word is introduced in the file, its repetition and highlighting are more likely.

The report was unfortunately referred to in other reports. Yet, Onions added a comment which was not repeated anywhere else in the file: "*Even at the early stages of his career it is likely that he could make a significant contribution to the Service.*"

Onions' report made no mention of the fact that he told Piotrowski at the end of the interview (after spending three hours) that he considered him to be *"head and shoulders above the other candidates"*.

Onions' report made no mention that Piotrowski inquired about whether his publishing an article about the *CSIS Act* would jeopardize his application and that he offered to cancel it if it would. Similarly, the report did not reflect that Onions told him to "*go ahead*" and publish it as long as he does not reveal he is an applicant.

<u>Goodale Report</u>

The file contained a report titled "Pre-Employment Security Interview" report and was prepared by Goodale after the meeting in April 1989.

In one of the opening paragraphs, Goodale suggested that Piotrowski was labelled a McCarthyist and fascist by his "fellow students". Even though Piotrowski described himself as centrist or slightly right of centre liberal democrat she wrote that he made some statements that could be interpreted as "extreme rightist". Not one of those statements which she considered to be potentially "extreme rightist" was reproduced. Coming with Onion's allegation that the intensity with which Piotrowski talked being "extreme", the file's tone was set.

I was shocked and disappointed when I read that. What I told her was that I had written an article in a student newspaper which prompted a critic to respond with a comment that no one would take me seriously who did not have a poster of McCarthy on their wall. I used that incident and the fact that left-wing student activists are prone to calling people they don't like "McCarthyists" and "fascists" as examples of some of the silliness that takes place on university campuses. Regarding her "extreme rightist" reference, I would have loved to know what statements she was referring to. I know what "extreme rightist" is. I never made any "extreme rightist" statements. Reading her comments raised the possibility that political ideologies and distinguishing between them were not her strong points. I found it a sad commentary that CSIS interviewers would feel that such clichés actually need to be dignified by being mentioned in my file and that some CSIS analysts would assume that because something was said and written down it must be true. Unfortunately, the nature of the initial article that I had written about discussing how the pacifists were promoting unilateral disarmament which was destabilizing and in the Soviets' interests was completely ignored by Goodale and other analysts. Instead of examining what I actually wrote, mud that was thrown at me in such a lazy fashion that I felt like I was back in university being pilloried by another lefty Anti-American. The fact that this was coming from a CSIS officer really surprised me. Sadly, she did not make any mention as a contextual reference to my having told her about my law professors who preached the abolishment of private property and revolution, or who described the police and CSIS as the greatest threat to our civil liberties.

In another paragraph, Goodale discussed the Montreal newspaper incident in 1984 that Piotrowski described involving an op-ed from Moscow consisting of Soviet propaganda and Piotrowski exposing its contents as falsehoods in a letter-to-the-editor. Goodale wrote that the Soviet author had been visiting Canada. She made a big deal about the letter and suggested that it "should be cleared up".

I never said that the Soviet author was visiting Canada. I don't know where she got that from. She muddled the facts. What was there to "clear up"? I answered all of her questions at the time. I had already shown the Soviet article and my letter to Onions and had copies at home. If Goodale or anyone else at CSIS wanted to see them again they could have asked and I would have gladly delivered copies.

Comment on Finances: In this section, Goodale suggested that Piotrowski was unable to provide a specific breakdown of how he accumulated his savings.

That was not true. I gave Goodale a complete breakdown of how I earned money through part-time and summer jobs since I was fifteen. I saved my earnings and invested in GICs. I then used all of what I had accumulated, along with a contribution from my father, to the purchase of a condo that I split with my girlfriend. I provided all the totals of my savings and the amount that the condo cost. What I could not remember was the specific bank book balance on specific dates. However, if it was necessary, I could have dug it up. I worked and saved my earnings in a disciplined manner. Instead of being recognized as a financially responsible individual Goodale's comment raised suspicion about my financial sources. Although I was proud of my financial acumen, she managed to make me appear like I either did not know what I was doing or was covering something up and unnecessarily cast further clouds of suspicion over my candidacy.

Incidentally, I told Mrs. Goodale that I had saved $2,500 while working at the Banff Springs Hotel during the summer of 1981, not the Palliser Hotel in Calgary in 1981-82 as she suggests and incorrectly calls the Pallister [sic]. Again, she muddled the facts.

In one paragraph of the report, Goodale stated that Piotrowski's article on CSIS in the ISI journal was published in November 1988.

That is incorrect. I gave a lecture at a conference about subversion in November 1988. The ISI Journal with my article about CSIS that I told her was forthcoming ended up being published after the interview in April 1989. Again, she muddled the facts.

In another paragraph just before the "Comment" section, Goodale wrote that before Piotrowski left Toronto at the end of May 1989, he called to thank her once again for the interview.

This statement is misleading and probably contributed to this notion throughout the file that my character is excessively "forceful". As an applicant to CSIS it occurred to me that it might be a good idea for CSIS, and the various departments working on my file, to know where I lived. The primary reason for my call was to tell her what my new address in Ottawa was going to be. I only thanked her again at the end of the conversation as a polite way of ending the call. The fact that I called to give her my new address was not even noted in her report. I thought I was doing CSIS a favour by providing it with information, and somehow it came out looking bad on me. Ironically, one of the investigators working on my security clearance in

*Ottawa was subsequently surprised to learn from one of my references that
I had moved to Ottawa.*

Assessment: in one paragraph Goodale suggests that Piotrowski
did not answer questions directly and that he used anecdotes. This
passage is referred to in other reports to suggest that Piotrowski was
trying to throw the interviewer off.

*There is no mention of the fact that Goodale told me to "talk" and only
guided me by giving me general topics to discuss. Nor was there any
mention of her own behaviour and that she was laughing like crazy. I used
several examples of statements of people with whom I disagreed to explain
my views and her almost uncontrollable laughter in fact encouraged me to
continue and pursue the train of thought. If she had not responded the way
she did I would have answered differently. I tried to adjust to what she was
looking for. The suggestion that I did not answer her questions directly or
otherwise is not true. I spent over four hours in the meeting with her giving
complete answers to her questions.*

In the report she suggested Piotrowski strayed off topic and had
to be reminded of the questions.

*I remember Goodale and I laughing so hard and so for long that
afterward I asked her on two or three occasions to remind me of her
question. Considering that the interview lasted over four hours this is not as
bad as she makes it out to be. Unfortunately, her own behaviour is not
mentioned at all in the report which makes the document a terribly
inaccurate reflection of how the interview went.*

Reliability: In one paragraph Goodale states that because some
students labelled Piotrowski a McCarthyist and a fascist, and because
he spent some time debating with Soviet apologists and anti-
Americans, she did not believe that he could be "relied upon to be
objective and rational in his work".

Welcome to the world of CSIS and its mindset. If one is critical of Soviet policies, Soviet apologists will label you all kinds of nasty things. That does not make them true. However, to CSIS internal security investigators such defamatory insults are truth and fact. And if they are truth and fact, then it follows that the target of the defamatory character assassination is incapable of being objective or rational.

How does being a student of political science engaging in discussions and debates and attempting to articulate a position in writing disqualify himself from being capable of objectivity and rationality?

Regrettably, neither Goodale nor the analysts who repeated her claim appeared to have actually read any of the material that I wrote. However, in my file there is a report to the Director General of Internal Security dated August 2, 1990, which recommends that I get the security clearance requested. In the report it says that the positions I take are well informed and reasoned and that I am analytical in forming and acting on my opinions. Regrettably, those words only appear once throughout the file and are drowned out by the other grotesque claims.

Suitability: In the suitability section Goodale wrote that Piotrowski has attained a high-profile level and that "he will experience great difficulty in adhering to CSIS policy with respect to Disclosure of Employment" policy if hired.

This was heartbreaking to read. There is no mention of the fact that I told Onions that I was planning on writing an article about the review of the CSIS Act and told him that I would be happy to cancel the project if there was a risk that it would jeopardize my application. There is no mention that Onions told me to "go ahead". Did all the other "high profile" people whom Onions told me were frequently hired by the Service have such difficulties? Why would I specifically be considered to have such difficulties? I asked Latrappe on several occasions as well and even had the Communications Branch vet my Review Committee submission, but Goodale had already made up her mind.

Loyalty: In the loyalty paragraph Goodale said that Piotrowski made some comment about the Polish Ambassador to the U.N. Unfortunately, the next sentence is blacked out, and then she stated that she thought Piotrowski was contradicting himself.

This was obviously in relation to my discussion of the Shevchenko and Spasowski books. However, what is clear is that she muddled the facts. I never mentioned any Polish Ambassador to the U.N. Shevchenko was a Soviet diplomat and the Under Secretary General of the U.N. Spasowski was the Polish Ambassador to the U.S.

I remember when I raised the two books during our meeting, I asked her if she was familiar with them and she nodded her head yes and kept nodding approvingly while taking notes. Now it appeared that in fact she had no idea what I was talking about. Considering the fact that these two diplomats were among the highest-ranking defectors from the East at the time who wrote excellent exposes of the KGB and the corruption of the Soviet system, it is a shame that she had no idea who I was talking about. I knew my stuff and did not make any contradictory statements. I wish she would have written down what she thought was contradictory. It seemed to me pretty obvious that she was confused and the matters I was discussing were over her head. If she had no idea who or what I was talking about, how could she possibly analyze the contents of what I said and conclude that there was a logical incongruity?

Then came the most stunning sentence so far in the Goodale report: "A serious concern which begs to be asked is whether the subject initiated his application for employment on his own accord".

My jaw dropped when I read that. I could not believe that she had a "serious concern" that a foreign intelligence service was using me as a spy in an elaborate scheme to infiltrate CSIS. She actually thought that and suggested that the matter "begs to be asked"! My grandfather was killed by the NKVD at Katyn and she thinks I would work for the KGB? To think that Goodale could state such a thing after more than four hours of interviewing me just goes to show what dreadful judgment she is capable of. What is it that could have prompted her to question whether I was working for the Soviets or any other foreign agency? I really wish I knew. I answered all her questions truthfully and unreservedly about myself and my views and opinions. The positions I took were all consistent with the Canadian Government's domestic, foreign and security policies. Is that what was suspicious to Goodale?

Recommendations: The recommendation suggested that Piotrowski be re-interviewed to determine how many people knew of Piotrowski's application to CSIS.

When Goodale asked me how many people had I told of my application, I replied that I had informed my parents, de Fougerolles and McNabb. My father subsequently told me he told a friend. I told Goodale that when I found out I asked my father to not tell anyone else and he got the message. If there was any suspicion about this CSIS could have asked my father about it during the four meetings he had at the CSIS Montreal regional office. However, the file does not contain a word about my father's four meetings with "Daniel". Instead, there is a cloud of suspicion that permeates the file suggesting that I am unable to abide by the "disclosure of employment" policy.

I absolutely agreed with that recommendation although not for the reason that she does. I thought I should have been re-interviewed by a more educated, intelligent, objective and fair interviewer. This was one of the worst documents in my file as it gives an incorrect impression of what was said and what happened. Unfortunately, many of the statements in this report were repeated over and over again throughout the file.

Goodale Telephone Report

The next document was a report by Goodale to the Director General written following a telephone conversation Piotrowski made to her (around July 1990) to inquire about whether she could tell him anything about the lengthy delay in obtaining my security clearance. In one paragraph she wrote that Piotrowski told her that Latrappe informed Piotrowski that the average length of time to process an applicant takes eight months.

This is incorrect. I never said that. What I did say was that according to the SIRC annual reports the average length of time to get a Top Secret security clearance was 8 months and mine had so far taken more than twice that long and I was still waiting. Goodale muddled the facts again. Although I had no idea whether such a misrepresentation had any effect on my application, if Latrappe and his superiors saw it, (and there is a handwritten note on the document saying that the matter was discussed with Peter B------), then it would be logical for him to conclude that I was making things up and talking nonsense behind his back even though that was not the case at all.

In paragraph 5 of the report Goodale suggests that Piotrowski was "extremely polite".

I spoke to her the same way as at their meeting in April 1989. In fact, during this conversation the exact same thing happened as during our first interview. She started laughing again. Of course, she did not mention her own behaviour. However, the difference and contrast between the two reports is astonishing. Previously she implied that I tried to throw the interview off and now I was "extremely polite".

<u>Calgary Investigator Report</u>

The next document appears to be a three-page investigator's report from Calgary.

The investigator's report was based on an interview with the bartending course instructor. In paragraphs 10 to 17 state that Piotrowski was opinionated, forceful, intimidating, condescending and had few friends. The investigator's comments stated that Piotrowski is intolerant and "turned off" others further suggested that Piotrowski would only be able to get along with a few select people in any group and there is speculation that "one could expect dissention [sic] in any office he was employed in."

This report's most damning components were unfortunately repeated throughout the file. It was based on a brief period of a five-week course in the Fall of 1981 when I was 19 years old and still a teenager! That period was not only a very brief period but was a complete anomaly in my life. I was going through a difficult period of recovery after my academically disastrous first year at university.

People typically mature and change as they grow older lose their rough edges. I certainly did. A while ago I came across the following passage written by historian Arthur Schlesinger, Jr. In the forward to the book Robert Kennedy in his own Words [1988]: "Striving to win his father's approval and love, he began to harden his personality. The inner sensitivity and vulnerability remained, but a protective covering formed over it. He became in these years the Robert Kennedy who burst on public notice in the 1950s: a cocky young fellow, opinionated, censorious, rigid, moralistic, prickly, disposed to tell people off and to get into heated arguments" [page XIV]. However, Schlesinger then goes on to say: "Under John's humanizing influence, Robert began to lose his intolerance and rigidity. He grew relaxed and rueful, acquired more ironic views of life, developed his wry, self-mocking humor, and in time displayed a charm against which newspapers editors soon warned their reporters" [page XV]. Unfortunately, none of the investigators or analysts at CSIS appear to have even considered the fact that most people, including me, tend to mature with time.

The statement in the report that I stuck out of the crowd was true. The other students were interested in having a good time and I was more concerned with world problems which just goes to show how I was in the wrong place.

However, the memo said nothing of my friendship with my classmate Sylvain Gagner. Although I spent two years in Calgary, there was no mention of my performance and getting along with the staff at the Palliser Hotel, the 400 Club, or the Glencoe Club where I had worked. After the bartending course I studied at the University of Calgary for a year and a half. Not a word was mentioned in the report about the circle of friends that I hung out with and whose company I enjoyed. As I read the report, I reflected on the two drunk cowboys in the bartending class unable to stand up straight in front of the urinals. I wish I had known that CSIS would be preoccupied with my relations with them as a factor in whether to hire me.

The memo contained no context about who were the others and the stage of my life that I was in at the time.

However, what I thought was the most revealing thing in the report was the investigator's statement that "one could expect dissention [sic] in any office he was employed in." The word "dissension" is spelled in English with an "s" and not a "t". A CSIS officer who could not spell the word was prognosticating about my being a guaranteed future source of dissent and disruption at CSIS. The word "dissention" [sic] was similarly repeatedly misspelled by other CSIS agents in a number of other documents throughout the file as if I was some sort of a "dissention [sic] time bomb".

Throughout the period of reform and transition of the Security Service from the RCMP to CSIS there was a lot of public debate about the topic. Was it really possible that after all the years of public debate about the Security Service's role in identifying subversion and being able to distinguish it from "lawful advocacy, protest or dissent" that CSIS officers would still not be able to spell "dissension"? And these guys were crystal ball gazing and predicting who would be expected to engage in "dissention [sic] in any office he was employed in"?

Regrettably, once again, this conjecture would be repeated throughout the file and highlighted by analysts as though it were fact and a red flag warning, without any supplementary material to put the brief (and unhappy) period of my life in context. However, I had worked in a number of offices and businesses since I was fifteen. I was never a source of dissension at any place of employment, including the hotel and clubs that I had worked at in Calgary. Regrettably, none of that was mentioned.

Just as was the case with Goodale's report, this one was inaccurate and judging by the frequent repetition of its contents was given a disproportionate amount of weight. Throughout the file other positive reports of interviews with people that I knew over a long period or with whom I recently worked and ignored and not quoted in any analyst's *assessment reports, while incorrect statements by one person who barely knew me for a few weeks nine years ago was considered more reliable.*

<u>Document #6</u>

The next problematic document in the file is a report from Calgary which says at the top: "To: HQ Region Security Screening". In one paragraph it stated that a search of the telephone directories failed to turn up Piotrowski's name.

Surprise! As I informed CSIS and repeatedly pointed out, during the period that I lived in Calgary between 1981 and 1983 I lived with my mother. After my mother had divorced my father, she legally reverted her name back to her maiden name which was Maria Adamska. I had provided the name to CSIS with my application. It would have helped if the "investigators" had looked up the correct name in the phone book. Something that should have been straightforward ended up being an unresolved matter.

Then there was another hiccup. When Piotrowski filled out his security clearance application forms he called his mother to ask her for the address number of the first apartment where they briefly lived in 1981 as he could not remember the apartment building number and could not find a record of it in his files. She told him the building address was 138 Glenview Avenue South West and that sounded familiar at the time. In fact, that was incorrect. The correct address was 1038 Glenview Avenue South West. Although Piotrowski had been contacted and asked if there was an error and corrected it after double checking, the details of the correction and Piotrowski's apology for the honest error are not noted. Instead, the investigator emphasized the error and suggested that Piotrowski was either sloppy or deliberately misleading.

<u>Document #8</u>

Memorandum dated 90-08-14; From: A/Chief, Personnel Security H.Q.; To: A/DG SIS.

This document appears to be a Memo from the Acting Chief of Personnel Security at Headquarters to the Acting Director General of SIS.

This document appears to be the summary comments by someone who saw Piotrowski's security screening assessment. It is full of the inaccuracies that plague the Goodale report. The whole issue comes up again about Piotrowski being a "McCarthyist". The report says that the label was "appended" to him. Again, the question is asked if Piotrowski could be relied upon to be "objective and rational" in his work with the suggestion being that this is doubtful.

This is an example of what happens when misleading or erroneous statements from an interviewer's or investigator's report are not sidelined and instead prominently highlighted by an analyst, and then copied verbatim into a memo from the "Acting Chief" of one unit to the "Acting Director General" of another. Although these false and hysterical characterizations were repeated and emphasized, nowhere was there any reference to Brandes' positive comments about my intervention at a conference or the contents of a paper I had written. Nowhere was there a reflection of the Communication Branch's commendation of my defending my assessment of the CSIS Act on national radio or the fact that the Communication Branch had reviewed my submission to the Thacker Committee. Instead, I could not be expected to be "objective and rational". That was right out of Goodale's report. What a contrast to the feedback I previously got from Finn and Kelly!

The next page begins by stating that it has been determined that Piotrowski's application to work for CSIS is well known "in the community".

What community? Where? The only people that I told were parents and the two people whom I asked for advice and a letter of recommendation. One report in the file stated that my co-workers while I was articling in Toronto for a full year actually thought I wanted to join the Justice Department. That was not repeated in any subsequent assessment or memo.

Then there is a reference to Piotrowski having attracted attention to himself and the suggestion that because he displayed a degree of above-average initiative that he would likely fail to adhere to the Disclosure of Employment Policy and that he would turn out to be a "loose canon" [sic].

In the context of the expression "loose cannon" the word is spelled "cannon", and not "canon". As with the case of the investigator and analysts not being able to spell the word "dissension" and predicting much of it throughout my future wherever I worked, this "Acting Chief" was predicting that I would be a "loose cannon", even though he too could not spell the word. Regrettably, the expression came up a few times in the file and was not spelled correctly once.

Again, there is no mention is made of my having contacted the Service each and every time I ventured to public something about CSIS to check whether it was OK or would be a problem. Not one word. Onions and Latrappe totally mislead me.

The next paragraph suggests that because Piotrowski displayed initiative during the five-year review period, he would be a source of problems for CSIS with regards to the *Privacy Act* and general security and cause "embarrassment to the Service".

The memo makes no reference to the fact that it was the Deputy Director of CSIS, Harry Brandes, who wrote to me to encourage me to bring my "perceptives" [sic] to the attention of the Thacker Committee. No mention is made that I checked with Latrappe before making the submission to confirm that it would not be a problem. No mention was made that I provided the CSIS Communication Branch with a draft copy and they vetted it and that they provided corresponding input.

Not only did I notify CSIS before the submission was made, but all of the material always stood up for CSIS. Never did I ridicule CSIS or attempt to embarrass it. No mention was made of Kaplan's assessment of my paper or either Finn's or Kelly's opinions of my testimony before the Committee.

When it comes to embarrassment, it seemed to me that the only cause of embarrassment was the way CSIS made a mockery of my application.

Concerning the idea that I would be a problem with regards to the general security of information, there was no basis for this speculation. Not only did I work in law firms where solicitor-client privilege is a sacred cow, but one report in the file by an investigator who interviewed people who knew me in recent years stated that I was discreet with personal information. Yet, this one observation was never repeated elsewhere by any analyst. There is no basis whatsoever for doubting my ability to keep my mouth shut. Yet, it's in the file. Throughout my lengthy career in the federal civil service I never had any problem regarding security of any information. At one point in my career my Secret security clearance was upgraded to Top Secret when my job required it without any problem.

The final paragraph says "as you know, this candidate has been most insistent in the pursuit of his candidacy". This adds to the overall impression that Piotrowski's personality was forceful.

In early 1990, a full year after his initial interview, I called Latrappe to ask him about the status of my application. Latrappe told me that the security clearance was being worked on and that he had regular meetings with the people who were working on it. He told me that if I wanted to get updated on the situation that Piotrowski should call him monthly. I did that. He then advised me that I could call semi-monthly and encouraged me to do this. There is no mention of any of that in the file. Instead, the file states that I am "most insistent".

Not only was my clearance taking more than twice as long as the average according to SIRC reports, but the latest SIRC report at that time actually stated that candidates who applied to CSIS a full year after I did, following the media recruitment blitz in September and October 1989, had already started training with CSIS the month before I was rejected. Having been told by Latrappe that the only thing holding up the offer was a security clearance, I was of course getting anxious. However, considering the circumstances I thought I was patient. Instead of telling me that I should call him for regular updates, Latrappe would have been more honest if he had told me "There's no point in calling me. Someone from CSIS will contact you if we have something to tell you."

<u>H.Q. Personnel Services</u>

This is a report which says "H.Q. Personnel Service Tracking Unit" at the top.

Under the heading "Introduction" it says "This report contains information that should be considered prior to any offer of employment with CSIS" and asserts that wherever Piotrowski worked it could be expected that there would be "dissention"[sic].

The report was a verbatim copy of passages from the Calgary report. Once again, an analyst who was unable to spell "dissension" correctly highlighted all the negative allegations against me and did not present any characteristics that could be potentially seen as "positive". Not one. Onions and the panel members who met me considered me "head and shoulders above the other candidates" and "the best" [to be discussed] of the Intelligence Officer candidates. But this analyst had a big warning flag that had to be considered before any offer of employment was made.

<u>Handwritten Memorandum</u>

The next document that was full of inaccuracies was a handwritten document of several pages entitled "K. PIOKOWSKY [sic] Prospective IO Candidate". This document appears to be the product of an "analyst" in the "Briefing Unit".

The first paragraph begins by stating that "after reading the pre-employment interview of Piokowsky [sic], almost every aspect of the interview militates against the hiring of subject."

It appears that all this "analyst" did was read the Goodale report and regurgitate all of the falsehoods that she put into it and in the process of "analysis" made a dreadful account of me appear even worse than the way Goodale did. I did not think that it would be possible, but I overestimated CSIS and its staff. I doubt that the person read the Goodale report more than once and certainly nothing else in my file. My name was continuously misspelled throughout the document as "Piokowsky".

Piotrowski's interest in national security issues was described as "obsessive". Then there is the suggestion that he was "garrulous" and that he was probably "using the tactic to confuse an inexperienced interviewer". The report then asserts that this propensity to talk "combined with vanity, which is surely the case" is enough to question Piotrowski's ability to abide by the secrecy rules at CSIS.

The only thing that made any sense in this report was the implication that Goodale was "an inexperienced interviewer". I never imagined that at a CSIS interview the interviewer would tell me to "talk", and that talking would be seen as a tactic and a symptom of vanity "which is surely the case". As I read through my file I realized that I was reading fiction and that Canada's intelligence agency was staffed with fiction writers.

The next paragraph merely repeated the other Goodale claims (outlined above) and the suggestion is then made again that Piotrowski tried to "throw the interviewer off".

No mention is made of the fact that Goodale told me to "talk" and that she began laughing at some of my description of my university experiences and kept on laughing throughout the entire interview. No mention is made of the effect her behaviour had in encouraging me to keep it up. She was obviously enjoying the interview and so was I. I never tried to throw any interviewer off.

The last paragraph on the first page contains speculation about Piotrowski hiding some contacts with Soviets. The file says that Piotrowski never mentioned any contacts with Soviet "delegations, representatives and individuals" while working at two hotels in Alberta. The analyst wrote that there "were many" such delegations and "it seems impossible that a person of his nature did not come into contact with some of these individuals". The suggestion is therefore made that Piotrowski was covering up something and that he likely made some contact with Soviet representatives.

This paragraph was in the same ballpark of fiction as Goodale's questioning whether I was a spy. As an employee in the hospitality industry I was comfortable offering food services to hotel guests. I was comfortable speaking with customers. However, when it came to people from the Soviet Union or other Communist countries, the average ordinary citizens of those countries were typically not able to travel in the West on their own. Any official delegations would be just that...official delegations. There was no point speaking with them about anything other than strictly business as they were watched and could get into trouble. In fact, I remember in 1976 being in at airport gate waiting area and the Soviet Olympic water polo team or some other swim team was waiting for another plane at the next gate. I remember attempting to speak with one individual. I just wanted to find out where they were from and how did they like their visit to Canada and stuff like that. I was hoping that perhaps they might speak English or French or that with my rudimentary Polish I might be able to understand some basic Russian. Unfortunately, my efforts were futile. It was simply impossible. The guy refused to engage in any attempt at dialogue. Why? It was obvious. A number of people on the team turned their heads and looked at us. The Soviet was being watched and could get into trouble. After my previous trips to Poland I perfectly understood that. If there ever were any Soviets who sat in my section of the restaurant, I knew that any communication had to be succinct and limited to the business of ordering and delivering their meals.

I wondered...how did this writer know that there "were many" Soviet delegations there at the time? I couldn't remember one single party that I served either as a dining room waiter, banquet waiter or room service waiter that was Soviet. I remember plenty of Americans, Japanese and Mexicans, but no Soviets. Even if there were however, the fact is that I simply had no contact with them. None. Period. The suggestion that this "seems impossible" makes me wonder whether the writer has ever been to the Banff Springs or Palliser Hotels. Both hotels are huge. I only came into contact with a small fraction of the hotel guests at any time. The paragraph, and others like it throughout my file lead me to believe that many people who dealt with my file had a remarkably fertile sense of imagination and may have suffered from debilitating paranoia. Ironically, in the psychological assessment I was accused of having "too many fears". A case of the pot calling the kettle black perhaps?

At the beginning of the next page there is a suggestion that because Piotrowski did not know what his mother's psychology M.A. thesis topic was any claim he may have to being inquisitive was "a joke".

I knew my mother obtained an M.A. in psychology before I was born. However, the fact that I could not specify what her thesis was about was all it took for CSIS to conclude that my claim to being inquisitive was a farce and a fraud. Welcome to the world of CSIS. I could not help wondering whether the "analyst" had any degree.

The second to last paragraph suggested that because Piotrowski debated political issues with students at university, he would probably cause problems with colleagues at CSIS.

I was exposed to the basic principles of logic by my father throughout my youth. I took a course at the University of Calgary in the Philosophy Department on the subject. Although discussion, including debating, are essential learning opportunities in social science courses in university, CSIS does not look favourably on such activity. It never occurred to me that voicing ideas and discussing them was problematic and that CSIS was so afraid of the concept and activity.

The last paragraph on that page suggests that Piotrowski is a security threat and that he would probably harm relations with other workers.

Labelling me a security threat was ludicrous. What is the basis for that? Ironically, there is a memo elsewhere in the file confirming that I was granted the Top Secret Security Clearance. In addition, the reports from the last two law offices where I worked suggested that I got along well with co-workers. These observations were never repeated and highlighted in any subsequent report. Why would I have had an offer to complete my articles at one law firm if I was "harmful"? How could I have had three separate contracts in 1989 and 1990 with Bob Kaplan, MP, and Senator Stanbury to join the staff of their offices if I was "harmful"?

The second paragraph of the third page says that Piotrowski "sounds pompous, arrogant and egocentric".

The person who wrote this never actually met me and did not appear to have read anything that I had written. It appears that the analyst read one report by an interviewer who was laughing for hours and the result is that I was "pompous, arrogant and egocentric". Later would I discover that CSIS thought I was even worse than that!

Paragraph 10 on the final page said that it is doubtful that Piotrowski could keep a secret. The next sentence stated that he has a "desire to educate other people" which would certainly upset fellow workers. Paragraph 14 again stated that Piotrowski is "unable to account" for his savings.

I never believed that it would be possible to say so many incorrect things in such a small amount of space. This stuff was getting painful to read. However, by this time I realized that this was not a serious and competent appraisal of my candidacy.

Document #9

This is a report which says "H.Q. Personelle [sic] Service Tracking Unit" at the top.

Under the heading "Introduction" it says "This report contains information should be considered prior to any offer of employment with CSIS".

Again! There is a verbatim copy of passages from the Calgary and Goodale reports. Again, it is said that where I worked it could be expected that there would be "dissention" [sic]. Again, the repetition of clairvoyance of rebellion to the point of saturation carpet bombing.

Panel Interview Report

The application file contained a number of documents relating to the panel interview. There were some notes written in French that were made after the interview. One stated that "La comité a des inquétudes tant qu'a la capacité du milieu à intégrer un individu d'une aussi forte personalité". Readers familiar with the French language may cringe at the phraseology used.

Why would the Service have any difficulty integrating someone with my personality? I did not have any difficulty integrating at any other previous place of employment before or since.

A related memo dated 89-07-10 stated that Piotrowski was found to be "the best" Intelligence Officer candidate by the panel and that he had scored 830/900 in the interview.

Onions told me that I was "head and shoulders" above the other candidates and now the panel found me to be the best candidate. Yet, their reference to my allegedly "forte" personality would be used in the memo to the Director as one of the reasons to reject my application.

<u>Briefing Note for the Director</u>

The file included a short memorandum addressed to the CSIS Director. Under the heading "individual's Background" it stated that Piotrowski was the author of several articles and briefs on CSIS. The next line said that Piotrowski participated in radio talk "shows".

In fact, I had only one article published in the ISI journal, made only made one submission to the Thacker Committee, and participated in only one radio program. The description of the volume of work is exaggerated. Nowhere is there is mention that I asked Onions and Latrappe every time if any of these events would be a problem and offered to unconditionally drop them.

Under the heading "Recruitment Information" the first piece of bad news is the psychological assessment which is negative. (The psychological assessment is discussed in the next chapter.)

The next thing it says is that the suitability interview from Toronto in June 1989, had some negative comments and they are blacked out. Again, there is the comment that Piotrowski had "few friends". The briefing note then says that all pertinent information about suitability was reviewed.

The bottom line in the briefing note is that Piotrowski was rejected because of his "forceful, inflexible and intolerant attitude towards others".

From the material which I was given I was flabbergasted by this statement. My file was dealt with in the most cursory manner with little attention paid to explanations or other points of view. One of the Calgary reports suggests that my case was only touched upon on four separate days, and these consisted of a few telephone conversations or looking up the wrong name in the telephone book.

A problem throughout the file concerns the methodology that was used. As far as I could tell, there are only two negative reports, Goodale's and the Calgary investigator's, as well as the awful psychological assessment. Yet, the people who reviewed these reports did not want to counterbalance the nonsense with anything else or place them in context. As a result, a "review" in fact consists of nothing more than "repetition" and the highlighting of negative points. Unfortunately, there seems to be a belief throughout the file that repetition constitutes a "review" and ensures truth and accuracy.

Regarding the "forceful, inflexible and intolerant attitude towards others" description, none of my bosses or co-workers at any place of employment since I started working at the age of 15 would ever say anything like that. Why would the law office where I worked in the summers of 1986 and 1987 offer me an opportunity to work for a year and complete my articles there after law school? If I was so disruptive, why would Bob Kaplan and Senator Stanbury hire me in 1989 and then again in two consecutive contracts in 1990?

I was puzzled by the statement that I am "inflexible". I wish the people who wrote and repeated this false allegation would have provided a single example. On every issue and topic, I have always been willing to listen to other evidence, and have often changed my mind. I have met many people over the years who have never admitted a mistake and never said sorry. I have never been one of them.

These gross generalizations about myself lead me to conclude that after 21 months of "investigating" my case CSIS really knew very little about me. In fact, the file is so horrible, that I would not even hire the person in question. The problem, however, is that I did not even recognize myself in it at all. It is not a file about me.

The Briefing Note went on to say that it is likely that Piotrowski would pursue every avenue to seek employment with the Service.

I knew the competition is tough and I could accept not being one of the best. I knew my limitations, and there are always other equally or better qualified candidates. Being rejected was not the problem. Being rejected for the reasons that were described was. Any self-respecting person would want to correct all the nonsense in his or her file if it consisted of inaccuracies.

The *Privacy Act* copy of the application file that Piotrowski was given contained no specific mention or analysis of any of Piotrowski's writings or transcripts of his speaking engagements which would have provided a contrast to the accusations of extremism and inability to be objective.

There was no discussion or analysis of any trend, evolution or development in Piotrowski's life. There was very little discussion of any of Piotrowski's friends and officemates, classmates at different stages in his life. None of the few discovered "facts" that could have been considered positive was ever repeated or emphasized. Instead, the primary and paramount emphasis was on one report from one bartending instructor from a brief period nine years prior and the Goodale report.

There was no mention of Piotrowski's contact with Brandes or his letter encouraging Piotrowski to submit his (non-extremist) views to the CSIS Act Review Committee.

There was no mention of Piotrowski's having worked for former Solicitor-General Bob Kaplan or getting positive feedback and encouragement from former CSIS Director Ted Finn or RCMP Deputy Commissioner W.H. Kelly.

There was no mention of the French teacher at CSIS having moved temporarily into Piotrowski's home.

There was no mention of Piotrowski's informing Onions on day one or repeatedly informing Latrappe of his writing and speaking opportunities and inquiring whether they would be a problem.

There was no mention of the Communications Branch reviewing Piotrowski's submission to the Parliamentary Thacker Committee.

There was no mention of Piotrowski's period of military training with the Royal Montreal Regiment.

There was no mention of the CSIS investigator from Montreal who visited Piotrowski's home as part of an investigation and no analysis of Piotrowski's responses to the questions.

There was no mention of Piotrowski's father's four meetings with a CSIS officer in Montreal.

There was no mention of Victor Goulet's assertion that Piotrowski's ISI journal article was "very good" or that according to Goulet, Piotrowski knew more about CSIS "than the people who work [t]here". But there was more to come.

CHAPTER 11:
MEETING THE
CSIS SHRINK SQUAD

The covering letter which Piotrowski received with the *Privacy Act* files stated that the psychological test results were not included in the release. If Piotrowski wanted to "consult the results" he could call a certain telephone number.

As the results of the psychological assessment appeared to have been negative and had an influence on the decision to reject Piotrowski's application, he promptly called the number and scheduled a meeting at a downtown office two days later.

On November 7, 1990, Piotrowski went downtown to a meeting at the CSIS offices to go over the psychological assessment which was not released to him with the *Privacy Act* package. By this time Piotrowski had two days to review and digest the package he had received. It left him stunned by the dreadful, insulting and humiliating portrayal of himself. However, it also left him shaken by the realization that the organization that he previously believed in and supported in different ways was not only staffed with seriously misguided and incompetent people dealing with the assessment of candidates, but the organization as a whole, including both the staff that met him in the recruiting process and those who "analyzed" the resulting reports, evidently disliked him so intensely that he was portrayed as a vain trouble-maker who would engage in "dissention" [sic] everywhere he went and was possibly a spy.

Piotrowski realized that the chances of the psychological assessment providing any redeeming or mitigating features to his failed candidacy were remote. However, for the sake of completeness and getting as much of an understanding of what happened, he felt compelled to attend the meeting.

As Piotrowski approached the building where the meeting was to take place, he noticed from a distance a number of people outside smoking. As Piotrowski got closer he recognized Gendron. When Gendron saw Piotrowski his face suddenly lit up and reflected a degree of excitement and happiness which was evident by his ear-to-ear smile on his face and the tone of his voice when he said "Hello Chris! Remember me? I'm Vincent and I'll see you upstairs in a few minutes!"

Piotrowski was somewhat surprised by his upbeat excitement. When Piotrowski first met Gendron during their first meeting the previous year, he was stone cold. Similarly, since moving to Ottawa Piotrowski had in fact bumped into Gendron on several occasions on the streets downtown and said "Hello" to him. However, Gendron's facial expressions on each of the occasions were always the same: stone cold. Gendron never responded with anything other than a nod and kept walking. Considering the circumstances under which they were meeting and the sadness that Piotrowski felt that day, he was truly stunned by Gendron's lack of sensitivity.

Shortly afterward Piotrowski found himself in the office of the CSIS chief psychologist, Larry Finch, who was supported in the meeting by Gendron. Finch was a middle-aged man who appeared to be very sure of himself. Piotrowski sat in a chair with his back to a wall while the two psychologists sat at angles in front of him effectively cornering him. There was a small coffee table between Piotrowski and the other two. The atmosphere was not a pleasant one. The two CSIS employees behaved as though they were being forced to meet with Piotrowski whom they treated as though he were a hostile adversary. They wanted nothing to do with him and were not keen to divulge anything to him, although whatever they revealed they did with relish.

Finch started by asking Piotrowski "Why are you here?" Piotrowski explained that he received a letter that said he could call a number to schedule an appointment to "consult the results" of his psychological assessment. Piotrowski wondered why Finch wanted him to explain this since Finch was clearly familiar with these details. Finch then said "You're not going to like this."

Finch had a file in his hands and told Piotrowski that it was his psychological report. Finch told Piotrowski that he was not allowed to see it, however, Finch could tell him what was in it. The only thing Piotrowski knows about its contents is what Finch chose to tell him. This is what CSIS meant by "consult the results".

Piotrowski asked if he could take notes. Finch replied "You can write whatever you want, but if you intend to take this matter to court I will deny everything".

I was shocked at what I had just heard. Not only did CSIS and its shrinks not understand me and my motivations, but I was hardly interested in any lawsuits. Finch's declaration that he would unhesitatingly perjure himself under oath and open himself to a criminal conviction because of his desire to suppress the truth left me almost speechless. I did not ask him whether he felt any discomfort at lying under oath as I did not want to aggravate the overall situation which he needlessly set up to be tense as if he was expecting a confrontation.

Based on one interview with Gendron and a few multiple choice and "true or false" written tests (and presumably seeing the various reports from people who met with him or investigators in the field but that was not confirmed), the "psychology unit" of CSIS came up with certain conclusions about Piotrowski.

Finch then told me that that there is nothing profoundly wrong with me, but I was less attractive than other candidates. He then told me that I had:

a superficial personality; narcissistic tendencies; a need of constant attention and admiration; and a somewhat exaggerated perception of myself within society and that there is nothing to justify it. Furthermore, I was: agitated and had too many fears; inner-directed; self-centred; insensitive to others, and generally had a negative impression of others and lacked empathy. The results of the writing test were supposed to have been "OK". The intelligence test results indicated that I was above average and between the 75th and 90th percentiles.

So there it was. According to this guy who never met me, I was a jerk, a monumental asshole, and a fraud. There were no positive or mitigating features in my character or personality worthy of mention.

I tried to remain cool and collected. In the span of just a few minutes, I felt he had been dealt some pretty unfair low-blows. Coming after receiving the disastrous application file package this was even more stunning than I anticipated. Even though I was stunned and somewhat in shock, I did not want to give either of those two guys the satisfaction of knowing how much they had hurt me.

Both Gendron and Finch sat like Cheshire cats grinning with the silliest of smiles that looked like they were sadists who were enjoying themselves. Finch then said to me "You must find this pretty shocking right now". The grin on his face precluded me from giving him an answer.

My mind was spinning trying to absorb what I had been told. The package I had received was full of errors and misrepresentations. I was expecting that this was going to be unpleasant. However, this assessment of me left me perplexed. I did not recognize myself in it at all. I don't recall ever being assessed with such conclusions either before or after. While I tried to figure out how they could have come to those nasty conclusions about me, my mind raced with images of Brandes greeting me with a smile telling me how I had asked the best question of the conference and Onions shrugging his shoulder and telling me that I was "head and shoulders above the other candidates". And now I was being told what a horrible person I was with no redeeming features. The previous high esteem that I held the Service in had just been deflated big time. I subsequently discussed these conclusions with a number of people who know me and the consensus is that CSIS got it wrong. Friends are obviously likely to say pleasant things, but people who have known me for many years told me they did not recognize me in their description. I did not either.

Finch then told Piotrowski that he had too much ambition and motivation to be happy at CSIS. He said Piotrowski should go "work for IBM". When Piotrowski asked what sort of people they were looking for he was told they did not want any "high-flyer" but people who were not preoccupied with where they are going. They were looking for people who were comfortable with themselves and content in being a cog in a machine. Finch stated that he predicted that in three years Piotrowski would not be able to deal with "the boredom and the bullshit" and that people like him who were allowed in the Service were not "happy campers" after a while. Finch even said that he would be willing to "eat my shorts" if Piotrowski would be happy there after just three years.

Gendron then spoke up and with a smile said that CSIS wanted people with "no pretense". In other words, he was telling Piotrowski that he was a phony. He said it with a smile.

Gendron then referred to the meeting I had with him and asked me whether I remember my trying to give him a copy of my published article about CSIS. He referred to it as justification for the above conclusions. I sat there stunned. How could answering a question about what my hobbies were and showing him a piece of my writing support the above conclusions? I hoped to get as much information as I could out of these two guys, and leave as soon as possible as this was an unpleasant situation and their behaviour and obvious glee throughout was aggravating. They displayed a lack of professionalism and were not respectful. If anything, their silly smiles gave me the impression they were mocking me.

However, as I reflected on what they were telling me, I was struck by examples that contradicted their conclusions. When they said that I had a need of constant attention and admiration, this was contradicted throughout the file that I had just received where it repeatedly implied that I did not care what others thought about me. In fact, both descriptions were incorrect. I certainly care what others think about me, but if I really was in constant need of attention and admiration, I would have pursued a career in acting and not one where I hoped to spend my life in some shadow of anonymity.

After my disastrous first year at the University of Toronto, I was proud of myself for my academic recovery, graduating from McGill with a B.A. Honours with Distinction with an "A-" average, getting into Osgoode Hall Law School, graduating, articling at a law firm, and completing the Bar Admission Course. Anyone who thinks that was easy has no idea. My life was not boring. At least, not to me. Like everyone else, I knew I had my own strengths and weaknesses. Yet, I felt I had reason to be proud. The suggestion that I had an "exaggerated" and "unjustified" perception of myself struck me as being unjustified.

I was tempted to ask where did these two guys get their degrees? I was really curious as to where Finch got his Doctorate. I wanted to make sure that if I had a child in the future who wanted to study psychology that I would advise them to avoid that particular school. A few years later I found out from a senior CSIS officer that Finch did not have a Ph.D. and only had a Master's degree in psychology. I did not get the impression his sidekick Gendron was any different in terms of education and professional qualifications. Neither was a Doctor of Psychology. The CSIS "Psychology Unit" appeared to be staffed by apprentices.

Piotrowski tried to keep a straight face throughout the meeting. Piotrowski did not want to give either of these men the satisfaction of seeing him upset by their "results".

Concerning the written tests, this component of the application process was reviewed by the *CSIS Act* Review Committee. The Committee's 1990 report *In Flux but not in Crisis* stated that the Service's psychological tests "may be inappropriate" and "they may have little, if any, predictive value with respect to who will develop into a good intelligence officer". No kidding.

Piotrowski left the meeting totally deflated. It would have been impossible to have considered his application having been more disastrously dealt with by CSIS. While he was eager to turn the page, there was still some unfinished business.

CHAPTER 12:
APPEALS AND
A CORRECTION

After having received the *Privacy Act* package with the redacted application file and having met with the CSIS psychology squad Piotrowski reflected on the contents of the package and what he was told.

On the one hand, Piotrowski was relieved that the process was over. After months of waiting for a final determination, Piotrowski finally had an answer. It was certainly not the one he wanted, but as the time to deliver the final verdict took so long, Piotrowski had increasingly suspected that this would be the outcome and was not surprised when it finally came. However, the contents of the package and the apparent reasons for the rejection bothered him. He could accept being rejected, but thought the reasons that were identified were inaccurate and unworthy of an organization in the "intelligence" business. Accordingly, Piotrowski followed up with three steps.

First, Piotrowski decided to prepare a document to submit for inclusion in his application file as a "correction" which was his legal right to do. He figured CSIS might be interested in some feedback on the investigation and analysis in this file. On December 12, 1990,

Piotrowski sent CSIS a 32-page correction document with the request that it be inserted in his application file.

Second, Piotrowski forwarded the correction to the Director and requested a review of his application. Piotrowski knew that the chances of the Director overriding his recruitment team were zilch, but he thought that if he did not try now, he would always wonder "what if?"

Third, Piotrowski sent a copy of his correction document to the Privacy Commissioner of Canada and requested that they review the redacted portion of what had been released to him to determine if anything that was redacted could in fact be released to him, along with anything else that was in the file and previously withheld.

Piotrowski subsequently found out during a meeting with Greywood that CSIS was conducting a review of how his file had been handled and their recruitment process. Apparently, Greywood had been asked some questions about his interactions with Piotrowski. Later Greywood would inform Piotrowski that in fact some changes had been instituted at CSIS in the application and recruiting process, although he could not tell Piotrowski what they were. Piotrowski hoped that it involved telling Latrappe and the investigators and analysts to be a little more objective, honest, truthful, reasonable and competent.

Piotrowski subsequently received a letter from CSIS Director J.R. Morden dated July 18, 1991, in which he wrote "[...] we have completed an exhaustive review of all documentation and information pertaining to your candidacy. Upon review of the many points you have raised, we have identified certain practices and procedures which could be improved upon to increase the efficiency and effectiveness of the recruiting process. We will act upon those in the coming months. As for the processing of your application, our review indicates that its rejection was established through the use of standard practices and procedures and adhered to the equity and merit principles. I am therefore satisfied that the Service dealt with your application in an appropriate and equitable manner and that the decision to reject your candidacy was the right one."

Once I received that letter from Morden any shred of remaining hope for joining CSIS was now effectively dead. The fact that my case resulted in a review and greater "efficiency and effectiveness" at CSIS was a remarkable admission that their system was less than optimal. However, the process was only part of their problem. The other problem was the judgment of the people involved in my file. The reference to "equity and merit principles" was a standard bureaucratic slogan. Yet, CSIS had its own version and meaning of those principles. How was it possible for me to be initially told that I was "head and shoulders above the other candidates" and dragged for so long through all the stages in the CSIS recruiting process and have the highest score at the final panel interview only to be rejected based on "equity and merit principles"? The Briefing Note for the Director in the Privacy Act package I previously received did not mention equity and merit principles anywhere.

About a year later I was walking down Bank Street in downtown Ottawa when I saw Latrappe walking on the sidewalk towards me. Latrappe was looking at the ground as he walked along the edge of the building on that block. I was walking toward the street edge of the sidewalk and maintained my head up while staring at Latrappe without saying anything. As Latrappe came closer towards me he suddenly raised his head. Latrappe instantly recognized me. His eyes bulged wide open as a terrified look spread across his face and his pace intensified. Latrappe quickly disappeared without saying a word to me. He took off like a chicken.

A week after Piotrowski sent his correction document to the office of the Privacy Commissioner of Canada he received a phone call and then a letter confirming that the Privacy Commissioner's office agreed to review the redactions that CSIS had made to his application file with a view to determining whether any further information could be released to Piotrowski.

Nine months later Piotrowski received a large brown envelope in the mail. It was about half an inch thick. However, the released information was largely the same material and did not contain any new revelations. At the same time, the member of the Office of the

Privacy Commissioner of Canada who worked on Piotrowski's file called to inform him that the psychological report could not be released. However, she informed Piotrowski that what was possible was for him to attend the CSIS offices again to see the document itself. The lady stated on the phone that she received a memo from Finch which she read to Piotrowski. Finch's memo included this passage: "the file was present during the meeting and it is our interpretation that Piotrowski had the opportunity to look at the test results. However, he did not express a desire to do so."

I was not surprised by Finch's statement that the lady read to me on the phone. He told me he would deny everything if I brought this matter to court. Anyone willing to lie under oath would presumably have no qualms with falsehoods under normal circumstances. Finch and his sidekick were being dishonest. What was it that they wanted to hide so much? Could it be that the divulgence of their methods could lead to an exposure of less than professional standards?

The lady made a big deal out of this new opportunity to "consult the results" again and made it sound like this was a special privilege. However, she discussed the opportunity with a sense of urgency and said that if I wished to take advantage of this opportunity to see the psychological report, I would have to contact the CSIS as soon as possible and preferably that same day or the next at the latest.

I pointed out to the woman on the phone that CSIS took two years to deal with my application, took the maximum allowed period under the Privacy Act of two months to produce my Privacy Act request initial package, and just took another nine months to produce what appeared to me a few additional documents containing nothing new. Accordingly, I thanked her for her work and for informing me of this latest opportunity to see more documents. However, I told her that I refused to be rushed and would take my time to determine whether to take advantage of the opportunity. When the woman on the phone realized that her attempt to prompt me into immediate action was unfruitful, she became discouraged and concluded with "do as you wish". "Thank you. I intend to" I told her. I did not follow up on seeing the document as the thought of seeing the grinning shrink squad again made my stomach turn.

Once my correction document had been sent to CSIS and my appeal to the Privacy Commissioner was over I was finally able to turn the page and move on. I put all my files and notes into a box and tucked them away in a corner of the attic. At the same time the Cold War, which sparked my initial interest in national security, appeared to be coming to an end. The Soviet empire and the Soviet Union itself disintegrated. The timing appeared to be fortuitous. It seemed an appropriate time to forget about that national security stuff and move on to new endeavours.

After receiving the rejection letter I immediately activated "Career Contingency Plan B" and plunged myself into searching for alternative employment. A few months later, on the same day, I was offered two separate positions by different government organizations. I picked the one that offered more long-term career possibilities. Life went on as if nothing had happened. When one door shuts, typically another one opens. Often, there is fortune in misfortune. It may not be obvious at the time, but eventually one sees the light as the fog clears. I certainly earned more money than I would have at CSIS, probably endured a lot less stress, and probably had more satisfaction. Eventually I had to admit that the CSIS rejection, which initially hurt, was actually a blessing. I eventually came to realize that they did me a favour by not admitting me into their ranks. For that, I came to be grateful. I just wish they would have been more professional in the treatment of my file and rejected the application at the beginning rather than taking two years to put me through the process before making up their minds. Unfortunately, their incompetent treatment of my application resulted in bitter memories. Every time I see a media story about another CSIS snafu I can't help wondering "What did they do now?"

In November 1991 I was invited by CBC Newsworld TV to participate in a live national program called "On the Line with Patrick Conlon". Two other journalists who had written negative books about CSIS were lined up to be on the program and the CBC wondered if I would join the panel to add a contrasting opinion. I was familiar with both books and thought this could be fun. It was a national call-in show that lasted 90 minutes. CBC flew me to Toronto and paid for my stay at a hotel as the program was broadcast on

Saturday evening. During the show, the two journalists made numerous claims about CSIS violations of civil liberties that sounded exaggerated and I challenged their arguments. The following Monday at work I got a call from Blair Dickerson, an assistant in the Solicitor-General Minister's office. He called me to congratulate me on the performance and to thank me. The following month I got a Christmas Card from his boss, the Hon. Doug Lewis. I assumed that was an illustration of the "merit principle" in action.

A few years later I decided to get rid of my national security library. I called CSIS to see if they were interested. They were. One of their librarians came over to see my collection and we negotiated a price for a sizeable portion. In October 1994 I received a letter from Debbie Cavana, Head, Acquisitions and Serials Management, Information Centre, stating "It was a pleasure to go through the collection – staff here are most pleased with the titles acquired." I guess the people employed in the "Acquisitions" department don't spend much time visiting used bookstores like some students do.

CHAPTER 13:
GETTING THE
TOP SECRET CLEARANCE

In 2008 Piotrowski was working in a unit of a federal Government department where the mandate was broadened from a previously economic one to include national security considerations. As a result, all the employees in the unit were required to upgrade their security clearances from "Secret" to "Top Secret". Piotrowski filled out the necessary forms and submitted them to the Department security coordinator. Many months later he received a phone call from a CSIS officer. The lady on the phone requested that he attend an interview with her at the CSIS headquarters building.

Piotrowski went to the CSIS building on Ogilvie Road in the East end of Ottawa on the designated day. He went to the Commissionaire's desk at the entrance and provided his name and the name and phone number of the agent with whom he was to have a meeting. He was told to wait. Shortly afterward the CSIS officer appeared and introduced herself as Lianne Thibodeau. She invited Piotrowski to follow her into a small meeting room on the ground floor which did not require him to go through screening to enter the secure area of the building. The meeting room was small and had a small table with two chairs on opposite sides. Thibodeau thanked

Piotrowski for coming and produced a recording device which she set up on the table between them. She explained that she needed to record the interview. He said that was fine. Piotrowski was all business-like and looking forward to getting this over with. It reminded him of the interviews he had with CSIS almost twenty years earlier but this time he had a better understanding of how CSIS misinterprets things and he was determined not to give them the chance to misunderstand whatever he would say. Thibodeau commented that Piotrowski appeared uncomfortable or nervous and asked him if we would rather postpone the interview. Piotrowski objected and said that he was not nervous in the least and he wanted to get this done now as previously scheduled. He insisted that not only the tape recorder between them be turned on but so should every other recording device, including any hidden cameras that were in the room.

Thibodeau asked Piotrowski a series of questions that he was already familiar with. At one point she asked him about his career. He replied that she probably saw his application file from when he applied to have a job like hers. She denied knowing anything about it and appeared surprised. At CSIS the left hand does not know what the right hand knows and vice versa (or knew before it destroyed the file).

I had to go over my background and I made it as simple as possible. I explained that I have been a Government civil servant since the year that CSIS rejected my application. I explained to her that in the 18 years that I had been a Government bureaucrat I never engaged in any behaviour that would be considered disloyal or a risk.

At the end of the interview, Thibodeau said "One last question. Are you aware of anything that would justify or prevent giving you the Top Secret security clearance?"

I responded by saying "Yes I do and I want to make sure that you record this properly and take accurate notes. There is nothing in my history or background or anything that I have ever done which would justify denying me a Top Secret security clearance. However, we are all human. You and everyone in CSIS are human. Humans make mistakes from time to time. CSIS occasionally makes mistakes. You will undoubtedly make several during your employment here. The only thing that could explain my not getting the Top Secret security clearance is that you and CSIS make a mistake on my file. CSIS already made a mistake in the treatment and rejection of my application almost twenty years ago. All I ask is that the next time you make a mistake, please make it on someone else's file and not mine. CSIS has already screwed me once and that's enough."

The woman's jaw dropped and she stared at me is disbelief and shock. She'd obviously never heard anything like it before.

Two weeks later Piotrowski got a phone message from Thibodeau. She indicated that he got the Top Secret security clearance.

CHAPTER 14:
CSIS ASSESSMENTS, PREDICTIONS AND LESSONS

Of the multiple blunders I made in my youth, there were three that really stuck out for me and which I regretted for a long time. First, I wish I had not bothered to study security and intelligence matters as much as I did. It is an interesting subject, but I could have spent much of the time pursuing other more rewarding interests.

Second, I wish I had not developed an interest in the RCMP's Security Service and CSIS. I subsequently discovered that my reverence for CSIS was unwarranted. I had overestimated the character of the institution and its employees. I had to admit, I was naïve.

Finally, my biggest blunder was that I had applied to CSIS to pursue a career as an intelligence officer. In hindsight, that was probably the stupidest thing I ever did in my life. If I could turn back the clock and undo just one thing in my life, it would probably be to tear up my application letter and resume before I mailed the envelope. I could have saved myself from a lot of grief.

A book by Peter Boer titled *Canadian Security Intelligence Service* was published in 2010. It has a few pages under the heading "The Hiring Process". The book suggests that there are many positions available to CSIS agents, and most require extensive education and world experience. Analysts are expected to have a minimum of a graduate degree, five years of experience in a particular field and a long list of scholarly publications in order to demonstrate a level of expertise in any specific discipline.

The application for Intelligence Officer positions "can take upwards of a year". CSIS supposedly recruits "the best available". Applicants must be Canadian citizens, have a post-secondary degree and possess a driver's license.

Boer seemed to base this part of his book on a 2003 interview with Emil Spilchak, apparently a former Prairie Region Chief of Human Resources. Spilchak indicated that the candidates may be invited to a series of four interviews. "We're looking for you to impress us," he said. A CSIS psychologist looks for more than just signs of depression or anxiety. "We're looking at the interview from the perspective of determining the person's motivation. We want to know if they're hiding something or if their motivation isn't genuine". Subsequent interviews are with two senior staff members and another with a member of the executive branch. Passing all of those will trigger a "massive background search of the individual's life, going back as far as 10 years. Agents seek out former employers, friends, teachers, neighbours and family members to determine if anything in the applicant's past could be used against them in the form of blackmail." It could be "a financial thing". If the background check comes back clean "a candidate is finally approved to be offered a job with CSIS". The average applicant can expect to wait 8-10 months before being offered a position.

Based on my experience, that description of the hiring process is misleading. As Finch told me in person, although he said he would deny it if he was ever asked to testify under oath, CSIS is not looking for "high flyers" or people who are preoccupied with where they are going. They are looking for people who are comfortable with themselves and content in being a cog in a machine.

Based on my experience with the CSIS interview process, the best advice that I could give to anyone who is thinking of applying for a job at CSIS is to apply elsewhere.

However, if you are really determined, then consider these tips which you may find helpful. Make sure you know the topic of your mother's M.A. thesis. Make friends everywhere. Don't discuss, debate or argue anything, anywhere, at any time. Be flexible. Don't give anyone the impression that you are intensely interested in anything. Avoid anything that may in any way be considered "extreme" to anyone. Never say anything positive about CSIS or negative about Russian foreign policy. Don't write or publish anything. Don't write any letters to the editor. Don't appear before any committees or on the radio. Don't speak at any conferences. Don't display any ambition. Don't say thank you in writing. Don't provoke laughter. Don't laugh yourself. Be succinct when answering questions in all your interviews. If told to "talk", do the opposite and be succinct. Ignore the provocations to keep "talking". Don't show the psychology apprentices anything. Memorize your monthly bank account statements. Don't earn, save, or invest too much money. Don't take any words of encouragement from senior executives or middle-ranking managers at CSIS seriously, especially if they suggest you make a submission to a Parliamentary committee. Whatever the agents in the recruiting process tell you about what you can do during the application process, don't believe them. Don't ever inquire about the status of your file. You get the idea.

CSIS investigators, interviewers, analysts, and psychology unit employees all made a number of negative assessments of me and nasty predictions about what would happen wherever I worked. So how did our "intelligence service" predictions turn out?

A few months after getting the rejection letter from CSIS I began a lengthy career in the federal civil service. I got married and raised a family. I pursued another graduate degree on a part-time basis. I was satisfied and comfortable in the positions that I had. I enjoyed the variety of moving every two or three years to a new position and doing different things. My annual performance evaluations were always positive. I received numerous citations and awards for my contributions to the work of the Branches where I was employed.

One of the highlights of my career was working at the Department of Foreign Affairs and International Trade. Over the span of several years I was given a diplomatic passport and frequently flew abroad as a Canadian representative at numerous international meetings. At one point a government office of a European country decided to host a "peer review" of their operations. They invited representatives from numerous countries on four continents to participate in the review. After the first day of meetings the hosts nominated me to be the Chair of the review committee. The exercise lasted several months and came to a successful conclusion.

I never argued with my co-workers or managers and never was a cause of any dissension or embarrassment. I was never "forceful" or "inflexible". I worked in public policy shops. Whenever a problem was identified we had to evaluate alternative courses of action before making a recommendation to management. In the course of working in groups and brainstorming I never clung inflexibly to any particular idea. I said what I thought and often changed my mind after hearing other evidence or more convincing arguments. Even if I felt one course of action was the best but others in the group or management preferred another course, I never made an unprofessional deal of it. I was never "intolerant towards others". I never did anything to jeopardize my Secret or Top Secret security clearance. I never divulged any information that was classified. I never had any financial "problems" and was not a spy. I have made my share of friends over my working life and keep in touch with a number of them since my retirement from the civil service.

I knew that the CSIS descriptions of my nature and predictions of "dissention" [sic] and being a "loose canon" [sic], etc. were nonsense.

Recent media reports indicating that 30% of recruits quit within five years suggest that CSIS recruitment "practices and procedures" may be in need of another review and corresponding adjustment in order to improve "effectiveness".

BIBLIOGRAPHY

Baltruweit, William J., *Down and Out in Canada's Intelligence Service: How CSIS used counter-intelligence techniques to investigate a depressed employee.* (Ottawa, 2000).

Boer, Peter. *Canadian Security Intelligence Service* (Folklore Publishing, 2010).

Cleroux, Richard. *Official Secrets: The Story Behind the Canadian Security Intelligence Service.* (Toronto: McGraw-Hill Ryerson limited, 1990).

Cole, Michael, J. *Smokescreen: Canadian Security Intelligence after September 11, 2001.* (New York: iUniverse, Inc., 2008).

De Pierrebourg, Frabrice and Michel Juneau-Katsuya, *Nest of Spies: The Startling Truth About Foreign Agents at Work Within Canada's Borders.* (Toronto: HarperCollins Publishers Ltd., 2009).

Frost, Mike and Michel Gratton, *Spyworld: Inside the Canadian and American Intelligence Establishments.* (Toronto: Doubleday Canada Limited, 1994).

Hamilton, Dwight. *Inside Canadian Intelligence: Exposing the New Realities of Espionage and International Terrorism*. (Toronto: Dundurn Press, 2006).

Kashmeri, Zuhair and Brian McAndrew, *Soft Target: How the Indian Intelligence Service Penetrated Canada*. (Toronto: James Lorimer & Company, 1989).

Kashmeri, Zuhair. *The Gulf Within: Canadian Arabs, Racism and the Gulf War*. (Toronto: James Lorimer & Company, 1991).

Kilgour, David. *Betrayal: The Spy Canada Abandoned*. (Scarborough: Prentice-Hall Canada Inc., 1994).

Maher, Donald G. *Shattered Illusions: KGB Cold War Espionage in Canada* (New York: Rowman & Littlefield, 2017).

Mitrovica, Andrew, *Covert Entry: Spies, Lies and Crimes Inside Canada's Secret Service*. (Toronto: Random House Canada, 2002).